Mom. The woman who followed her dreams and required me to do the same. You're the Kool Thing. This book is for you.

```
        ** Kitchen Printer **

by Jesse Hoffman

        Order #15-501
------------------------------
1    Character
     >CORONA (47)

1    R3 - Crispy Rice
     Salad
     >Works Sausage

1    R2 - Sorrel Rice

1    R2 - Ricotta Toast
     >Blackberry
------------------------------
     10/11/15, 10:22:25 AM

        Order #15-501
```

~ MARA   Kill fucking
          GORDON!

```
          ** Kitchen Printer **
Order #10-783
by Jayme Darling

     Walk-in 10:31 AM
-------------------------------
1    Character
     >ESCALERA (7)

1    R2 - Sorrel Rice
     >Bacon
     >no Hot
     >no Feta
     >no Egg
     Note: Radish on the
     side

1    Kabocha Socca
     Pancake
     Note: No arugula,
     yogurt on the side,
     not too well done,
     side butter

1    Open Food
     Note: Side maple
     syrup

1    French Toast
     >Maple syrup

2    Side Egg
     >Fried
     Note: No salt or
     pepper
-------------------------------
     4/20/16, 10:31:53 AM

     Walk-in 10:31 AM
```

Modifications politely accepted

Everything I Want to Eat

Sqirl and the New California Cooking

Jessica Koslow

with Maria Zizka

with a foreword by Lynda Obst

Photography by
Claire Cottrell
Jaime Beechum
Nacho Alegre

ABRAMS, NEW YORK

FISH *152–175*

Salmon with sorrel pesto
Stone crab fried rice with its mustard and kumquat
Squid toast
Grilled ridgeback prawns with piri piri sauce
Fried sturgeon with tartar sauce
Baccalà flower pot
Pickled sardine mezze platter
      Kohlrabi tzatziki
      Quick-pickled red onions
Black cod ceviche with purple yam and aguachile
Beet-cured salmon

JAMS *182–201*

Raspberry cardamom jam
Blenheim apricot and its kernel jam
Strawberry rose geranium jam
Shady Lady tomato and coriander jam
Spiced Gravenstein apple butter

DRINKS *238–259*

Brown rice horchata
Cascara tea
Chicory cloud
Ginger molasses cinnamon shrub
Lait 'n' egg
Orange-vanilla soda
Rhubarb lemonade
Turmeric tonic
Vanilla bean limeade
Avocado cardamom smoothie

LARDER *260–269*

Aioli
Almond hazelnut butter
Almond milk
Crème fraîche
Everyday mustard vinaigrette
Southern-style fresh cream
    and black mustard dressing
Green goddess dressing
Fermented jalapeño hot sauce
Magic green sauce
Schmearable "ricotta"

DESSERTS *202–237*

Flaky-ass biscuits
Hazelnut financiers
Valrhona fleur de sel chocolate cookies
Coconut rice pudding with lemon curd and coconut croutons
Carrot-ginger black sesame loaf
Powerballs
Malva pudding cakes
Hazelnut torte with raspberry jam, ganache, and toasted
    meringue
Upside-down cake
Sticky toffee whole-wheat date cake
Cardamom doughnut-ish tea cakes
Pecan frangipane and rhubarb tarts
Graham crackers
Lemon verbena peach pie

When I think of Sqirl, I think first of the mythical neighborhood food gathering spots of song, like Alice's Restaurant. "You can get anything you want at Alice's Restaurant." And of course that's true if what you want is turmeric tonic and a sorrel pesto rice bowl with feta (and lacto-fermented hot sauce), or rhubarb lemonade with buckwheat pancakes made from cactus flour. Of course I didn't know I wanted these things until I started coming to Sqirl every Saturday and Sunday morning at 8 am to beat the line almost four years ago. Since then, I've been meeting with a growing Saturday breakfast club. By now I've come to love these weekend morning talk-fests so much that I've set my iPhone alarm to make sure I don't miss a minute. There at Sqirl, the bunch of us—a prosecutor, a violinist/librarian, a movie producer (me), and assorted actors, writers, and . . . smart people—discuss crime, music, politics, and just about everything else on this green earth every other Saturday breakfast club in Iowa might discuss except that we are in Silver Lake, the hipster part of LA—a hotbed of late nighters and risers—and the place is jammed with a line around the block and we are gabbing away highly caffeinated at the crack of 8.

Lynda Obst, Sqirl Family

A great restaurant makes a neighborhood. And a neighborhood is defined by its favorite restaurant. Located in a particularly squirrelly and as yet ungentrified part of our nabe, Sqirl retains the things we east-siders love about the east side: Funkiness, a downtown NYC urban decay mixed with haute cuisine you don't have to dress for. (Also it's hard to find, like a test.) Its coffee is better than in Milan, whether it be a cup of Joe, cappuccino, or exotic hot beverages that fit perfectly in the hood, with a healthy twist: e.g., vegan horchata made from Koda Farm brown rice and Medjool dates. (!) Really.

At Sqirl, we look at each other's orders and comment, even if the diner sitting across from us is a stranger who then isn't any longer. "Oh, I love the brown rice porridge, it's the best ever. You're having the crispy rice salad? Next time order the house bacon with it. You never tasted bacon like this." Also, I might add, I accidentally eat healthily at Sqirl. I can't help it. Even the bacon is healthy.

And the line! The extravagantly down-dressed regulars fresh from the manhole/wormhole that connects Sqirl with its compatriot foodies in Brooklyn. There are newly arrived Japanese with a list of baked goods to buy from some inspired tour book mixing with movie and tech locals and their self-costumed children, all of whom I now know. You can get anything you want at Sqirl. Including a brand-new family of people who all live near you and know what you like to eat for breakfast. And if you ask sweetly, we share.

Lynda Obst

Citrus party at Mud Creek Ranch in Santa Paula, CA

"A cookbook is an incredible snapshot in time of cultural context and personal story. In this case, against a restaurant backdrop. And that's what is interesting to me. Learning about the cookbook author through their food and voice. The good ones are unafraid to be opinionated."

Friday, February 19th at 2:45 pm. Evan Kleiman in conversation with Jessica Koslow

Hands please

68 degrees and falling. Trenchcoat weather.

Ron Cornelsen was a peach

Dawgs of Sqirl

The menu reads:

FRIENDLY OTHERS

WHITES

SHAKEN W/ SSO $5.50

$3.50

ORANGE BLOSSOM HONEY
ORANGE BLOSSOM HONEY

CHA – COLD $6.

IRO YRUP $4.75

VEGAN HORCHATA $4.
MADE W/ KOKUHO BROWN RICE
& ORGANIC MEDJOOL DATES

VALHRONA HOT CHOCOLATTE $4.

ADDITIONAL ALMOND MILK $1.

MOUNTAIN VALLEY STILL or
SPARKLING H₂O ½ L $2.75

LAURA PALMER $5.00
PART RUBY GRAPEFRUIT
PART BAI HAO TEA

Yasmine Khatib ponies up at the bar

INTRODUCTION

In 2011, I started a jam company called Sqirl in a tiny corner space on the edge of Los Angeles's Silver Lake neighborhood. At first it was just me and one employee, Ty Swonger, squirrelling away to the sounds of Sonic Youth's "Jams Run Free" on volume LOUD. We had daily jam sessions. The following year, when I expanded Sqirl into a café, I wasn't sure people would find me. The sidewalk in front is in rough shape. There is no convenient place to park, which, in LA, matters a lot. And yet, people do come.

Every day, Sqirl closes at 4 pm. We put the same care and attention into breakfast and lunch that most restaurants direct toward dinner. Why shouldn't breakfast and lunch be just as refreshing and inviting?

HOW I BECAME THE GIRL BEHIND SQIRL

In 2005, after earning a master's in communications from Georgetown University, I moved to Atlanta.

They begin their days with an almond milk cappuccino or a fresh-pressed turmeric tonic. They stop by for lunch and order a wedge of daily quiche, sorrel pesto rice bowl with fixings, or maybe some kabbouleh (see page 85) to go, if they are in a rush. In the afternoon, they come for our rotating selection of baked goods: from the pillow-soft Valrhona fleur de sel cookies to the malva pudding cakes with oozy insides and crystallized crusts. Depending on the season, they might find spiced apple butter, strawberry rose geranium preserves, or Blenheim apricot jam to take home in a jar or, if they prefer, to enjoy spread over a slab of brioche toast.

Everyone was asking me what I was going to do with my life. The truth is, I had always wanted to cook.

Then came a life-changing meal at Bacchanalia, Anne Quatrano's James Beard Award–winning restaurant. I went home and immediately sent Anne an embarrassing email, pleading with her to hire me. We still laugh about it. I would wash her floors and caramelize a thousand apples a day for a chance to work in her kitchen. Somehow, it worked. She hired me the next day.

I started on Anne's pastry team. I remember one morning shift when I was tasked with baking black-and-white cookies, a classic Jewish deli treat—but these were anything but traditional. They were a southern version, cakey in texture, with a crunchy white glaze and dark-chocolate finish. That's when it hit me: This was a restaurant where the food is truly experiential. It wasn't just southern food; it was food influenced by Anne's travels and all the things she had eaten. Anne must have sampled a black-and-white cookie in New York and then come home to Atlanta to decipher her own playful version of it. Working in her kitchens, I learned to be unafraid to bring my own life experiences into my work.

Years later I was transferred to LA, where I continued working as a digital producer and defining integrated show content for clients such as Apple and Coca-Cola. I missed the kitchen, and I knew I had to figure something out. I took an overnight-shift job baking bread at the Village Bakery. Exhausted? Check. Happy? Absolutely.

My heart just wasn't in producing. It was like trying to fit a size 7½ foot into a size 6 shoe. I moved back to Atlanta to work with Anne once again, this time at Abattoir. Pretty quickly I started to develop an idea

I found my way through all of Anne's restaurants. Each one has a unique style and certain level of formality. Cooking at Quinones taught me how to always have the next idea for a dish ready. At Star Provisions, I realized that food has to be visually delicious—people eat with their eyes. At Bacchanalia, I learned what a perfect bite means.

What I wasn't expecting to learn from working at Bacchanalia was how hard it is to make a living in the restaurant business. I felt intense pressure to put my graduate degree to use, and I became convinced that New York was where I needed to be. So I put on a Dolce & Gabbana suit and scarf, hired a headhunter, and landed a job at Fox.

about the kind of cooking I wanted to do, what I could produce that would actually be my own. At Abattoir, preservation was the core of the restaurant. There were pickles everywhere, house-made charcuterie hanging from the ceiling, and far more jars of chutney and relish than I could count. That kind of cooking is truly southern—preserving out of necessity, but also striving to make food that is quietly nuanced. I would come home at night and try out my own take on preserves. Before long, I was working with my partner, Scott Barry, on designing jar prototypes.

On New Year's Day of 2011, I moved back to LA and started working in a kitchen adjacent to the Hollywood Farmers' Market, where we would receive leftovers from the market and preserve them for use in the kitchen. In March of that year, Sqirl launched. I rented a small kitchen five minutes from home in an area that seemed invisible unless you knew to look for it. Here I tinkered, making preserves with unique produce sourced from nearby family-owned farms. I formed relationships with those farmers—they have now become my extended family—and I fell in love with the diversity and beauty of California produce, especially its rare and unusual fruits.

I started with jam because, well, it was what my budget allowed for. I paid myself very little and put everything back into the pot, knowing that one day I wanted to have something more than jam. When that day came, I knew that what I made had to flow with jam. Breakfast and lunch fit the bill. Jam and raw bar? Not necessarily the closest match.

I was working in a tiny eight-hundred-square-foot space, with crates of fruit everywhere and not a lot of room to make much more than jam. So I made toast and jam. Then I found the most incredible rice, an heirloom variety grown on California's oldest family-owned and family-operated rice farm. Using that rice, I added a gluten-free option to my menu. I wanted something punchy and bright that would be a lighter choice, a savory breakfast option.

Eventually, I bought the market next door. I had a real walk-in fridge and was able to widen the menu to include refined, technique-driven terrines and cured fish. These were things I had wanted to do, expressive dishes beyond the traditional salad and sandwich that I could now make with the extra space. It started pretty much like that.

I know subrecipes and recipes on other pages that you have to flip to can be frustrating for the home cook. But hey, this is exactly how we make it at Sqirl. And I really want anybody to be able to re-create these dishes and enjoy them at home with friends. What I'm giving you is the real deal, although I have scaled down the quantities of ingredients because I'm guessing you want to cook enough for your family, not a Saturday brunch rush.

That said, you should feel free to just make one or two parts of a recipe. Maybe you like the look of Stinging Nettle Cavatelli with crispy spigarello and garlic (page 103), but making fresh pasta is not on the agenda for tonight. I get it. Just stop by the store on the way home after work and pick up premade cavatelli or gnocchi. Then, once you're home, set about making every other part of the dish really shine.

I live in LA, where everyone is known to be obsessively health-conscious and where dietary restrictions are the norm. People are always coming into Sqirl and ordering dishes with all sorts of substitutions and modifications—hold the feta, please, add extra kale.

In many ways the food at Sqirl actually suits this style of eating. The Sorrel Pesto Rice Bowl (page 63), for instance, is made up of a foundation of brown rice tossed in sorrel pesto, and it comes topped with preserved Meyer lemon, a silky poached egg, just a dab of lactofermented jalapeño hot sauce, and French sheep's milk feta, plus watermelon radish for both

crunch and garnish. But you don't have to have all those things on your rice bowl if you don't want them. You can get it vegan by ordering "The Stella" (named after my buddy Stella Mozgawa). I like to add kale to mine, but others may tack on avocado, breakfast sausage, cured bacon, or prosciutto. You can imagine the ticket calls. "R2 Meat Lover's with kale and avocado, no feta, hot on side." It happens.

I have to constantly think about ways to modify dishes for certain diets, which in a way has made me a better, more adaptable cook. Throughout this book, I provide notes that show how just about any dish can be modified for specific tastes and dietary needs. Similarly, I've included tips on how to change dishes depending on which vegetables look best at the market. If you want to make the frittata but don't have a carrot, try making a verdant version with whatever greens you do have in your crisper.

Play with these recipes. Empower yourself to taste as you go along, to adjust and season along the way. The more you taste, the more you will trust your ability to combine and shape these dishes into, yes, everything you want to eat.

A KEY TO THE RECIPES

V = Vegetarian

VV = Vegan

GF = Gluten Free

VO = Vegetarian Option

VVO = Vegan Option

GFO = Gluten-Free Option

Hold on to your hats, it's Janicza Bravo and Brett Gelman

Eggs & Toast
20—49

When I was first trying to figure out what kinds of eggs I might like to serve at Sqirl, I kept thinking about that video of Jacques Pépin cooking an omelette. You've probably seen it. It's from his first cooking show series, the one that aired on PBS. He begins by saying there are two ways to cook an omelette—the American way and the classic French way. Because he's Jacques Pépin, he kindly says that one is not better than the other. But then he goes on to show how to make an American omelette, cooking it until the eggs are completely set and the bottom is brown. Next he shows the French way and turns out onto his plate the silkiest, supplest, sexiest omelette with no crispy bits whatsoever. I think it's clear which one is the winner. And toast? Yes, always.

FRIED

Preheat the oven to 375°F (190°C). Set an oven-safe pan over medium heat. We use French de Buyer iron pans that are naturally stick-resistant because they are coated in beeswax. At home, nonstick or well-loved cast iron would work. Slide a pat of butter into the pan and let it melt. Before the butter browns, crack in a few eggs. Once you cannot see the pan through the white, move the pan to the oven. Finish cooking the eggs until the yolks turn bright golden and the whites are set but not totally firm, 3 to 4 minutes. Make sure the white part nearest the yolk is cooked through. At this point, if you prefer hard-fried eggs, use the corner of a spatula to break each yolk, then flip the eggs over and pull the pan out of the oven. Leave the eggs in the pan for a minute or so, until the second side has cooked. Even for a hard-fried egg, I don't like crispy bits. I want the whole thing to be soft and tender. Don't forget to season with fleur de sel and freshly ground black pepper. (The same technique works for one egg, or two eggs, or however many eggs will fit in your skillet.)

POACHED

Fill a pot with 2 inches (5 cm) of water. Heat until barely simmering. Add 1 teaspoon of white vinegar, which will encourage the proteins in the egg white to coagulate. Swirl the water to create a gentle whirlpool. Crack an egg into a teacup, lower the teacup into the swirling water, and let the egg slide out into the center of the whirlpool. Cook until the white is fully set, 3 to 4 minutes. Using a slotted spoon, transfer to a warm plate. Season with a pinch of fleur de sel and a crack of black pepper.

SOFT-BOILED (NOT SHOWN)

Fill a small bowl with ice water and add some fine sea salt (for seasoning the cooked eggs). Bring a small pot of water to a steady, gentle boil. Pull eggs straight from the fridge and, using a spoon, lower them into the water. Start a timer for 7 minutes. For the first 1 to 2 minutes, use the spoon to swirl the water into a whirlpool, which will give the yolks a chance to get centered within the shells. Turn down the

heat so that the water is bubbling away at a champagne simmer. Once the timer goes off, transfer the eggs to the ice bath and let cool for a few minutes. Crack and remove shells underwater.

SCRAMBLED

Crack a few eggs into a bowl and beat hard with a fork to really aerate them. The color should lighten a little. Season with fine sea salt (one pinch per egg). Slide a pat of butter into a nonstick pan set over low heat. Once the butter has melted completely, pour in the beaten eggs. Use a rubber spatula to scrape constantly and quickly along the bottom of the pan. There shouldn't be any dry or browned bits, but if you do get some stuck to the pan, don't try to pull them back into your beautiful silky eggs with the spatula. Cook until there are lots of soft little curds and the eggs look sort of like ricotta, scrambled but not fully set, about 2 minutes. Move the eggs to a plate (or, better yet, onto a piece of toast), because if you leave them in the hot pan, they'll keep cooking.

OMELETTE

Follow the same procedure for the scrambled eggs right up to the point where there are lots of little, soft curds. Then, remove the pan from the heat and tilt it away from you. Rap the pan on the counter so that the egg mixture settles on one side. Run the tip of your spatula around the edge of the pan and push any egg from the side closest to you over toward the far side. Use the spatula to roll the thin side over itself toward the middle, as if you were rolling up a carpet. Rap the pan on the counter once more to force the far side to come up the lip of the pan, then use your spatula to roll the far side toward the middle of the omelette. Now you should have an omelette shape with a seam running down the center. Invert it onto a warm plate.

Daily quiche

Daily quiche

This quiche is one of the first things that Sqirl's pastry chef, Meadow Ramsey, made at the restaurant. Every part of it is so super delicious: the flaky crust, the pillowy light filling, and the rich flavors of egg and cream. Since there's a good amount of eggs and cream, use organic ingredients. Don't skimp!

Makes 1 (10-inch/25-cm) quiche; serves 8 (V)

FOR THE CRUST

2 cups (250 g) all-purpose flour
¾ teaspoon fine sea salt
11 tablespoons (150 g) unsalted butter, cut into pieces and chilled
6 tablespoons (90 ml) ice water

FOR THE FILLING

½ small shallot, thinly sliced
1 or 2 cloves garlic, finely chopped
2 tablespoons extra-virgin olive oil
4 cups (80 g) spinach, chopped
1½ cups (360 ml) heavy cream
4 large eggs
2 large egg yolks
¾ teaspoon fine sea salt
Freshly ground black pepper
¾ cup (85 g) crumbled feta cheese
3 tablespoons chopped fresh chives

MAKE THE CRUST

Combine the flour and salt in a large bowl. Using the tips of your fingers, quickly pinch and smash the butter into the flour mixture. Once there are no butter pieces larger than a pea, drizzle in 4 tablespoons (60 ml) of the ice water. Still working quickly, toss to incorporate the water. Add 1 to 2 more tablespoons of ice water, toss, and try grabbing a small handful of the mixture to see if it'll hold together as a shaggy dough. If it doesn't, add a tiny bit more water and try again. Once it does, shape the dough into a disk, wrap in plastic, and place in the re-frigerator to chill for at least 1 hour or up to 1 week.

On a floured surface, roll the dough out to an approximately 14-inch (35.5-cm) circle that's just under ¼ inch (6 mm) thick, sprinkling the dough with additional flour as needed. Drape it inside an ungreased 10-inch (25-cm) springform pan with 3-inch (7.5-cm) sides, pressing to create an evenly thick crust. (The dough won't come all the way up the sides of the pan and it might want to flop over, but just press it gently against the sides of the pan until it holds its shape.) Place the pan in the freezer to chill for at least 20 minutes.

MEANWHILE, PREHEAT THE OVEN TO 350°F (175°C)

Remove the pan from the freezer, cover the dough with a piece of parchment paper, and pour in something to weigh down the paper and hold the dough in place while it bakes. (We use cheap rice; you could use pie weights, dried beans, or something similar.) Bake for about 1 hour, until the crust edges peeking out from under the parchment paper look golden brown. Remove the weights and paper and let the crust cool (but keep the oven on).

WHILE THE CRUST IS BAKING, MAKE THE FILLING

In a large skillet over medium heat, cook the shallot and garlic in the oil until softened, about 1 minute. Add the spinach and cook, stirring constantly, just until wilted. Transfer to a large bowl and let cool.

Once the spinach has cooled off a little, add the cream, whole eggs, egg yolks, salt, and lots of pepper. Whisk until well combined, then gently stir in the cheese and chives. Pour the filling into the baked crust. Return the pan to the oven and bake until the quiche quivers cohesively, like one piece of Jell-O (except it's not Jell-O; it's a delicious quiche), 30 to 40 minutes.

Let cool completely before slicing into wedges.

Store any uneaten quiche, covered with plastic, in the refrigerator for up to 1 day. To reheat, remove the plastic, cover with a piece of aluminum foil, and warm in a 325°F (160°C) oven for about 15 minutes.

HOW NOT TO OVERCOOK QUICHE

If this quiche soufflés, then it's overcooked. If it is completely set all the way through, then it's also overdone. You want to pull it out of the oven when a tiny 2-inch (5-cm) island in the middle is not quite cooked. As the quiche cools, the residual heat will cause that island to coast gently toward done.

PLAY AROUND WITH FILLINGS

The eggs and cream make up the base. Everything else is up for grabs. That's why we call it the "daily quiche." Instead of spinach, feta, and chives, try using onion jam (page 31), all the leftover cheese pieces you have in your fridge, and tons of herbs. Or use roasted potato, cheddar, and chives. You want to put bacon in your quiche? Sure—just cook the bacon until crisp, then crumble it in. You can use the leftover bacon fat to sauté greens and then add those in as well. Or quickly sauté sliced summer squash in a skillet over high heat until it browns, then add it along with dehydrated cherry tomatoes, fresh basil, and feta. In general, make sure all the ingredients are well mixed, although you should try not to smash the soft things.

Self-proclaimed quiche expert, Nicole LaLiberte, reporting for duty

Vegetally versatile frittata

I can never say no to the delicate, herb-flecked frittata that Russell Moore makes at Camino in Oakland, California. I also adore this version we serve at Sqirl, where vegetables and herbs are blended into a smooth puree that adds vibrant flavor, color, and, well, vegetables to the egg mixture. You can make the puree with almost any vegetable you like and feel the freedom to add freshly chopped herbs, such as tarragon, into the egg mixture.

Makes 1 (6-inch/15-cm) frittata; serves 1 very hungry person or 2 modestly hungry people (V, GF)

1 large (3½-ounce/100-g) carrot
2 tablespoons extra-virgin olive oil
Fine sea salt
¼ teaspoon ground cumin
3 large eggs

1 tablespoon unsalted butter
Fleur de sel
½ lemon
Hot sauce, for serving (optional)

FIRST, MAKE A CARROT PUREE

Clean the carrot—you can peel it or just wash it well (I don't peel). Slice it evenly into coins ¼ inch (6 mm) thick. Even is key.

Add 1 tablespoon of the oil to a small pan set over medium heat, then add the carrot coins and stir to coat them in oil. The goal: gently caramelize—not burn—the carrots. Add a pinch of salt, reduce the heat to medium-low, and cook, stirring often, until the carrots are tender all the way through, about 5 minutes.

Let cool for a minute, then transfer to the bowl of a food processor fitted with a metal blade. Add the cumin, another pinch of salt, and the remaining 1 tablespoon oil. If the carrots are having difficulty turning into a soft puree, add 1 teaspoon water just to get things moving. (Instead of using a food processor, you could mash the carrots with a fork.)

NOW, FRITTATA TIME

Preheat the oven to 350°F (175°C).

Crack the eggs into a bowl and add 2 pinches of salt. Whisk to break up the eggs, then whisk in the carrot puree.

Melt the butter in a 6-inch (15-cm) cast-iron skillet over medium-high heat. Add the egg-carrot mixture, stir for 15 seconds with a rubber spatula, then move the skillet to the oven. Exactly 8 minutes later, check in on the frittata. It should look slightly puffed (like a soufflé) and feel firm (not jiggly and wet) around the edges. If it needs another minute, leave it in the oven until it's just cooked, but take care not to overcook it. The middle will be the last part to finish cooking and, as you get the hang of it, you'll see that if you take the skillet out of the oven when the middle is still a tiny bit jiggly, the residual heat will finish cooking it.

Finish with a pinch of fleur de sel and a squeeze of lemon juice and serve with hot sauce and any of the following additions if you like:

ADDITIONS

During spring, I like to top this frittata with thinly sliced breakfast radishes and an herb salad made of parsley, chives, and opal basil. In the summer, we top it with the season's finest cherry tomatoes, halved and tossed with basil, dill, lemon juice, olive oil, and fleur de sel. In the fall and winter, thinly shaved kohlrabi makes a fine crunchy topping.

FEELING GREEN?

Prepare a verdant puree in lieu of the carrot. To do so, fill a bowl with ice water. Drop 2 big handfuls (about 70 g) of spinach, chard, or kale leaves (no fibrous stems) into a pot of boiling salted water and blanch for 1 minute. Transfer the greens to the ice bath. Let cool, then drain and squeeze out excess water. Using a food processor or a blender, puree the greens along with 2 tablespoons olive oil, a small handful of fresh herbs such as parsley and tarragon, and a pinch of salt. Instead of seasoning with cumin, try freshly grated nutmeg for warmth/holiday feelings. Or simply let the greens be their own subtle flavor.

FEELING MELLOW YELLOW?

Alternatively, you can cook sliced summer squash the same way you cook the carrot coins. Use the same amount (about 100 g). Instead of ground cumin, add a pinch of ground turmeric for color and 2 tablespoons finely chopped fresh herbs such as tarragon, basil, chives, or mint.

WHAT'S THAT? NOT EVERYONE HAS A 6-INCH CAST-IRON SKILLET?

You can make this frittata in a larger pan. Use an oven-safe one. Make the frittata as described and check to see if it's done cooking in the oven after 4 minutes. Depending on the size of your pan, it could take 4 to 7 minutes.

Green eggs and (onion) jam

Green eggs and (onion) jam

The Dr. Seuss toad in the hole.

Serves 6 (VO)

FOR THE ONION JAM

3 Vidalia or white onions (1 pound/455 g total)
3 tablespoons extra-virgin olive oil
2 tablespoons Worcestershire sauce **(see Note)**
1½ teaspoons red wine vinegar, or more to taste
½ teaspoon sugar, or more to taste
Fine sea salt

FOR THE CREAMED GREENS

2 tablespoons extra-virgin olive oil
2 tablespoons finely chopped yellow onion
Fine sea salt
1¼ cups (300 ml) heavy cream
½ bunch (225 g) spinach, stemmed
½ small bunch (110 g) green kale, stemmed

FOR THE GREEN EGGS

6 (1-inch-/2.5-cm-thick) slices country-style
  bread
4 tablespoons (½ stick/55 g) unsalted butter
6 large eggs
Fine sea salt
4 cups (80 g) arugula leaves
Extra-virgin olive oil
½ lemon
Fleur de sel
Freshly cracked black pepper

MAKE THE ONION JAM

Cut the onions in half through their north and south poles, then trim both ends. Peel away any papery layers. Set the onion halves, cut-side down, on the cutting board, with the trimmed end sides lined up in front of you, then slice the onions thinly. (I know this seems like way too much detail, but it's important that the onions are cut a certain way so that they cook evenly.)

Heat a Dutch oven or a large heavy-bottomed pot over medium-low heat. Add the oil, then add the onions. Cook, stirring occasionally, until evenly golden brown, about 30 minutes. It takes forever, but you can sort of set it and forget it, coming back every so often to scrape the bottom of the pot and make sure the onions aren't burning.

Add the Worcestershire sauce, vinegar, and sugar and stir well to combine. Reduce the heat to low and cook for another 10 to 12 minutes, scraping the bottom as needed, until the mixture starts gliding around the pot as one single clump. Season with salt and add a tiny bit more sugar or vinegar, if the onion jam doesn't taste sweet or tart enough. This is your moment to test your palate—look for a good balance of sweet and tart, like a pianist and a bass player rocking out in unison. Transfer the onion jam to a heat-safe container and let cool.

MAKE THE CREAMED GREENS

Heat a large pot over medium heat. Add the oil, onion, and ½ teaspoon salt. Pour in the cream, bring to a simmer, and cook until the cream is pale yellow and thick, about 6 minutes.

Meanwhile, drop half the spinach into a large pot of salted boiling water and blanch it for 30 seconds. Drain in a colander.

NOW GET YOUR WORKSPACE READY

You'll need to move fast in a moment to keep the greens green. Fill a bowl with ice and set another bowl on top of the ice. Have your blender nearby and ready to go.

Once the cream has reduced, add the remaining uncooked spinach to the pot. Right when you see it start to wilt, transfer everything to the blender, stuff in the kale, and blend. If the kale isn't incorporating into the mix, stop the machine and use a spatula to push down on the kale. Immediately pour the blended greens into the bowl set atop the ice so their color remains vibrant.

Once the blanched spinach has cooled off, use your hands to squeeze out all the liquid, then chop the spinach into thin ribbons and stir them into the cold kale mixture. Taste, adding a bit more salt if needed.

ASSEMBLE THE GREEN EGGS AND JAM

Preheat the oven to 350°F (175°C).

Using a biscuit cutter or shot glass, punch out a hole from the center of each slice of bread. Spread a thin layer of onion jam on the bread and on the punched-out piece as well. Spoon some creamed greens over the onion jam only on the bread slices (not on the punched-out pieces).

Heat two wide, oven-safe skillets over medium heat and melt 2 tablespoons of the butter in each. Place the bread slices flat in the skillets and nestle the punched-out pieces wherever they will fit around the slices. Crack an egg into the hole of each slice and season with a pinch of sea salt. Once you can't see the skillet through the egg whites, transfer the skillets to the oven and bake until the egg whites are set but the yolks are still runny, 5 to 7 minutes.

While the toasts bake, toss the arugula in a bowl with a drizzle of oil, a squeeze of lemon juice, and a sprinkle of fleur de sel.

Once the eggs are done, slide each toast onto a plate, pile the arugula salad to the side and a little on top of the toast, leaving the egg peeking out. Set the punched-out piece of bread on top of the toast (or hide it underneath the salad and make it a surprise!). Season everything with a pinch of fleur de sel and a few cracks of pepper and serve.

VEGETARIAN OPTION

Most Worcestershire sauce is not vegetarian (check the ingredients list for anchovies). To make this dish vegetarian, substitute 1 tablespoon of soy sauce.

Green eggs and (onion) jam

Lizz Wasserman is on the hunt for LA's breakfast scene

Famed ricotta toast

burnt brioche with house-made ricotta and seasonal jam

This is the blintz of my Katella Deli, post–Sunday school youth, in toast form. It's just missing a cream soda and a corned beef sandwich. And a nap.

Serves 2 (V)

2 tablespoons unsalted butter, melted

2 (1-inch-/2.5-cm-thick) slices brioche

⅔ cup (165 g) ricotta (page 268 or store-bought)

6 tablespoons (90 ml) of your favorite jam

Fleur de sel

Brush the melted butter on both sides of the brioche slices. Heat a large, heavy skillet over medium-high heat for 2 minutes. Place the brioche in the skillet and set a small weight on top. (A little pot or rame-kin works nicely.) Toast the brioche until golden brown, about 1 minute. Flip, reapply the weight, and toast the second side for 60 seconds or so. Remove from the heat. If you do not like the taste of char, you can always skip the next step.

Using tongs, hold each toast over an open gas flame until it has char marks, about 5 seconds per side. You want to lightly burn the brioche without drying it out too much.

Set the burnt brioche slices on two plates. Spoon what looks like a ridiculous amount of ricotta (⅓ cup/80 g per slice) on top, spreading it so that the edges are taller than the center, where the jam will go. Pour the jam in the center and let it pool lavishly. Finish with a pinch of fleur de sel.

NOTE ON BUTTERING

We butter the brioche on a tool called a butter wheel. It costs around $20 and it is definitely worth investing in if you are a real toast aficionado and want to make the best toast.

NOTE ON TOASTING

The brioche slices are too thick to fit inside most standard toasters. If you have a toaster oven, that's really the way to do this. If you don't have a toaster oven, then you should use a skillet to toast the brioche as described here.

SAVORY VARIATION

We also serve a savory version of this ricotta toast. In this iteration we do not burn the toast. To make it, cook about ¾ cup (110 g) shelled English peas in salted simmering water just until tender. Smash or puree half the cooked peas. Toss the other half with a few spoonfuls of mint salsa verde (page 107), then mix in the smashed peas. Spoon this over the ricotta. Top with small fresh mint leaves, a bit of grated lemon zest, a squeeze of lemon juice, plus a little more salsa verde (because why not?).

Jam-stuffed French toast

Jam-stuffed French toast

Sqirl started as a jam company, so priority #1 at the restaurant is to create a jam vehicle headed for your mouth. This one works quite well.

Serves 2 (V)

2 (1½-inch-/4-cm-thick) slices brioche
2 tablespoons Strawberry Rose Geranium Jam
    (page 196) or other not-too-thick jam, plus
    more for serving
3 large eggs
¼ cup (60 ml) heavy cream
1½ teaspoons granulated sugar
½ teaspoon fine sea salt
2 tablespoons unsalted butter
Confectioners' sugar
Whipped crème fraîche (page 265)
½ lemon
Fleur de sel

Preheat the oven to 350°F (175°C).

Use a thin knife to cut a slit 2 inches (5 cm) long through the side of each slice of brioche, creating a pocket where the jam will be able to reside. Open the slit with your fingers and spoon about 1 tablespoon of the jam into each slice.

In a large bowl, whisk together the eggs, cream, granulated sugar, and salt for several minutes, until voluminous and pale yellow.

Heat a large, heavy skillet over medium-high heat for 1 minute. Toss in 1 tablespoon of the butter and then, while the butter melts, dunk a slice of stuffed brioche into the egg mixture, pressing gently to ensure both sides are soaked with the egg mixture. The brioche should be soft and supple but not so soaked that it is falling apart. I usually count "1-Mississippi, 2-Mississippi," then flip and repeat on the second side. Place the brioche in the hot skillet and cook for about 1 minute on the first side.

Peek under the toast. Once it is nicely browned, flip it and pop the skillet into the oven for 4 to 6 minutes, until browned on the second side. Transfer the toast to a warm plate and repeat the dunking-and-cooking process with the second slice of brioche. (You could also do this with two skillets at the same time, if you prefer.)

To serve, sift confectioners' sugar everywhere, all over the toast. Top each toast with a dollop of crème fraîche (using a spoon that is first dipped into a bath of hot water so that you get that nice quenelle shape, if you want to be fancy) and a spoonful of jam. (I use red jams because Sqirl science shows that kids and adults alike respond with more excitement to red jams.) Finish with a squeeze of lemon juice and a pinch of fleur de sel.

NOTE ON BRIOCHE
Step one is to find the butteriest, most egg-rich brioche available.

The grown-up kid, part 1
ganache and nut butter toast

This might be the most decadent, heavy recipe in the book. It reminds me of gorging on a container of Nutella and then cursing myself afterward for not wanting to take back those wonderful, devious moments. I always want to pull this toast off the Sqirl menu, but then I think about adults ordering it for their kids—or for themselves—and it stays.

Serves 4 (V)

½ cup (120 ml) heavy cream
4.2 ounces (120 g) semisweet chocolate (I like Guittard's 58% cacao)
4 tablespoons (½ stick/55 g) unsalted butter, melted

4 (1½-inch-/4-cm-thick) slices brioche
¾ cup (195 g) Almond Hazelnut Butter (page 264)
Fleur de sel

MAKE THE GANACHE

Pour the cream into a small pot and slowly heat it up to just under a simmer. Chop the chocolate into chocolate chip–size or smaller pieces. (A serrated knife is a great tool for this job.) Put the chocolate in a heat-resistant bowl, then pour the scalded cream over the chocolate and set aside for a few minutes.

Sam Stewart, sweet dreams are made of this

Starting from the center of the bowl and working your way out to the edges, whisk quickly but gently to unite the chocolate and cream. Let cool to room temperature, whisking occasionally, about 30 minutes. (It'll thicken as it cools—you could pop it in the fridge to speed things along.)

NOW THE TOAST

At the point when the ganache has some nice body but is still pourable, brush the butter on both sides of the brioche slices, making sure to completely coat every inch. Toast in a toaster, toaster oven, or skillet until golden brown.

Dollop 1 to 2 tablespoons of the almond hazelnut butter on the opposite edges of each piece of toast, then smear the dollops toward each other to the middle, smoothing so that there's slightly more nut butter around the edges of the brioche and a little crater in the center. Spoon 2 to 3 tablespoons of the ganache into each crater, letting it pool. It's okay if the ganache drips over the edges of the toast.

Sprinkle a generous pinch of fleur de sel on each toast.

Eat decadently.

CRAVING ANOTHER WAY TO FEEL LIKE A KID?

For hot chocolate, stir 3 tablespoons ganache (and 1 teaspoon sugar, if you have a sweet tooth like I do) into a steaming cup of frothy milk. I like to add 1 tablespoon of malt powder into mine as well—takes me back to my Ovaltine days.

The grown-up kid, part 2
toast with jam and almond hazelnut butter
(aka NB&J)

Serves 4 (V, VVO)

4 tablespoons (½ stick/55 g) unsalted butter,
   melted
4 (1½-inch-/4-cm-thick) slices brioche
¾ cup (195 g) Almond Hazelnut Butter
   (page 264)
½ cup (120 ml) jam of any kind (see pages
   182–201 for ideas)
Fleur de sel

Brush the butter on both sides of the brioche slices, making sure you cover every inch. Toast (in a toaster, toaster oven, or skillet as a last resort since it dries the bread out a bit too much) until golden brown.

Dollop 1 to 2 tablespoons of the almond hazelnut butter on the opposite edges of each piece of toast, then smear the dollops toward each other to the middle, smoothing so that there's slightly more nut butter around the edges of the brioche and a little crater in the center. Spoon about 2 tablespoons of the jam into each crater and gently spread it out. Try not to mix—you want the jam to float on top of the nut butter.

Sprinkle a pinch of fleur de sel over each toast.

VEGAN VARIATION
Substitute baguette for the brioche, and brush it with olive oil instead of butter.

Beets on fish on beets on fish

tartine of smashed beets, smoked whitefish schmear, and beet-cured salmon

Every day we put a whitefish tartine on the menu. The smoked whitefish schmear itself stays constant, but the accompanying components change. This recipe is the latest iteration that has worked well at Sqirl. If you don't feel like making all the different components, you could just make the smashed beets or the whitefish schmear and enjoy it on or off toast.

Serves 4

Melted unsalted butter, for brushing

4 (½-inch-/12-cm-thick) slices country-style bread

1 cup (230 g) Smashed Beets (recipe follows)

1 cup (190 g) Smoked Whitefish Schmear (recipe follows)

12 slices Beet-Cured Salmon (page 175)

1 Persian cucumber, very thinly sliced

¼ cup (13 g) chopped dill

Dehydrated Trout Skin (recipe follows)

½ lemon

Fleur de sel

1 teaspoon Pickled Beet Powder (recipe follows)

Brush a friendly amount of melted butter on both sides of the bread, then toast in a toaster, toaster oven, or skillet until golden brown. Spread about one-quarter of the smashed beets across each piece of toast, then spread about one-quarter of the whitefish schmear on top so you can still see the smashed beets peeking out around the edges. Layer a few slices of salmon on each toast, arranging them in an undulating pattern. Into the crevices, stick the cucumber slices, dill, and pieces of dehydrated trout skin. Squeeze some lemon juice over the salmon and sprinkle with fleur de sel. Place each toast on a plate and finish by sprinkling a good pinch of pickled beet powder on each toast and around the edge of each plate.

Smashed beets

Makes about 1 cup (230 g)

3 beets (12 ounces/340 g total), scrubbed
¼ cup (60 ml) extra-virgin olive oil, plus more as needed
Fine sea salt

Freshly ground black pepper
1 teaspoon caraway seeds
1 clove garlic, peeled
½ lemon (optional)

Preheat the oven to 425°F (220°C).

Rub the beets with a bit of oil, sprinkle with salt and pepper, and wrap individually in aluminum foil. Put on a rimmed baking sheet and roast until they can be easily pierced with a fork, 40 to 60 minutes, depending on their size. (If the beets are different sizes, remove each as it is done.)

Once the beets are cool enough to handle, peel and trim them. Cut into large pieces, then put in the bowl of a food processor fitted with a metal blade and process to a puree. While the blade is spinning, slowly drizzle in 2 tablespoons of the oil. If the beet puree isn't as smooth as you'd like it, continue blending and drizzling in the remaining 2 tablespoons of oil.

Toast the caraway seeds in a dry pan over medium heat, shaking the pan often, until fragrant, about 4 minutes. Transfer to a mortar and grind to a powder. Add the garlic and ½ teaspoon salt, then smash to a paste. Mix this caraway-garlic paste into the beet puree. Taste, adding a bit more salt and a squeeze of lemon juice, if needed. Store in a covered container in the fridge for up to 3 days.

Smoked whitefish schmear and dehydrated trout skins

I really enjoy the word *schmear*. It's very comforting.

Makes about 3 cups (575 g) schmear and two 8 by 3–inch (20 by 7.5–cm) skins

1 cinnamon stick
1 teaspoon whole black peppercorns
1 tablespoon fennel seeds
6 allspice berries
2 bay leaves
¼ cup (50 g) sugar
½ cup (120 g) coarse sea salt or kosher salt
4 cups (960 ml) ice cubes

1 whole trout (about 7 ounces/200 g), gutted, head and tail intact, skin on
½ cup (65 g) finely chopped red onion
½ bunch (50 g) fresh dill, finely chopped
¼ teaspoon celery seeds
1 cup (240 ml) crème fraîche (page 265 or store-bought)
½ cup (115 g) aioli (page 263)
1 lemon, halved
Fine sea salt and freshly ground black pepper

In a small, dry skillet over medium heat, toast the cinnamon stick, peppercorns, fennel seeds, and allspice until fragrant, about 4 minutes. Transfer the toasted spices to a pot and add the bay leaves, sugar, coarse salt, and 4 cups (960 ml) water. Heat, stirring just until the sugar and salt dissolve, then remove from the heat. Add the ice cubes and let them melt.

Once the brine is completely cool, pour it into a wide nonreactive container and lower in the fish, making sure it's fully submerged. Cover and chill in the refrigerator for at least 3 hours and up to 12 hours.

Remove the fish from the brine, blot dry, and place on a wire rack set inside a rimmed baking sheet. Transfer to the refrigerator and let air-dry, uncovered, overnight. The fish will develop a sticky, shiny surface.

Now you're ready to smoke. Set up a smoker with your favorite soaked wood chips—we like to use citrus, oak, or pecan wood. Start slow, with very low heat (150 to 200°F/65 to 95°C), and keep some ice water in the smoker's tray at all times. The

fish is done when it reaches an internal temperature of 135°F (57°C). The trout will be lightly golden on top and will flake easily. Start checking the temperature after 20 minutes; thick trout could take up to 2 hours.

Peel the skin off the fish, keeping it as intact as possible. Spread the skin pieces flat on a tray and dry them in a dehydrator at 135°F (57°C) overnight or until crisp. Dehydrated trout skins can be stored in an airtight container at room temperature for at least 1 week.

Pick the fish meat off the bones and transfer to a bowl. There should be about 6 ounces (170 g). Stir in the onion, dill, celery seeds, crème fraîche, and aioli. Taste, then season with as much lemon juice, salt, and pepper as you like. Smoked whitefish

schmear can be stored, covered, in the refrigerator for up to 2 days.

NOTE ON SMOKING

You can also use a grill to smoke the whitefish. If you have a smoker box, fill it with wood chips soaked in water. If you don't, wrap soaked wood chips in a few layers of aluminum foil and poke lots of holes in the foil. Set the smoker box (or the foil pouch) on the hot side of the grill and set the fish, placed on a rack set inside a rimmed baking sheet, on the cool side. Close the grill vents. Check the internal temperature of the fish after 15 minutes, as this method takes less time than a smoker set to low. It's done when the trout flakes easily.

DON'T FEEL LIKE SMOKING YOUR OWN WHITEFISH?

Buy some. You'll need about 6 ounces (170 g).

Pickled beet powder

Makes about ⅓ cup (50 g)

2 beets (8 ounces/225 g total), scrubbed

1 cup (240 ml) distilled white vinegar

Trim and peel the beets, then cut them crosswise into slices ¼ inch (6 mm) thick, or grate them, if that's easier. Put the cut beets in a nonreactive bowl.

Bring the vinegar to a boil in a pot, then pour it over the beets. Let the beets pickle until the vinegar has

cooled to room temperature, about 3 hours.

Drain, reserving the beet-colored vinegar to use in place of red wine vinegar.

Lay the pickled beets on a tray and dry them in a dehydrator at 135°F

(57°C) until crisp, about 16 hours.

Drop the dehydrated beets into a high-speed blender and blend, starting on the lowest setting and increasing speed gradually, until you have pickled beet powder. Beet powder can be stored in an airtight container at room temperature for a month.

Avocado toast

Avocado toast

pickled carrots, garlic cream, house spice mix

Mark Bittman came into Sqirl and said, "Oh, of course you have avocado toast." And yeah, of course we do. We're in California. We're surrounded by avocados, and they are delicious. So, the question for us is really, how do we make avocado toast special enough that maybe Mark Bittman would want to eat it? Our response has been to take an expected staple and turn it on its head.

Serves 2 (V, VVO)

FOR THE GARLIC CREAM

1 to 3 cloves garlic (depending on how much you like garlic), minced
½ small shallot, minced
2 tablespoons fresh lemon juice
Fine sea salt
½ cup (120 ml) crème fraîche (page 265 or store-bought)

FOR THE SPICE MIX

½ teaspoon dried oregano
½ teaspoon white sesame seeds
½ teaspoon ground sumac

FOR THE AVOCADO TOAST

Melted unsalted butter, for brushing
2 (½-inch-/12-mm-thick) slices country-style bread
1 small ripe Hass avocado
Pickled Carrots (recipe follows)
1 scallion, thinly sliced on the diagonal
½ lemon
Fleur de sel

MAKE THE GARLIC CREAM

In a bowl, combine the garlic, shallot, lemon juice, and ½ teaspoon salt. Let the garlic and shallot soften for about 10 minutes. Fold in the crème fraîche, then taste and season with a bit more salt, if needed. Lightly whip until fluffy with body but still soft and spreadable.

MAKE THE SPICE MIX

Stir together the oregano, sesame, and sumac.

ASSEMBLE THE AVOCADO TOAST

Brush a friendly amount of melted butter on both sides of the bread, then toast in a toaster, toaster oven, or skillet until golden brown.

While the bread toasts, cut the avocado in half. Remove and discard the peel and pit. Set the avocado on a piece of parchment paper and cut each half lengthwise into thin slices. Cover with another piece of parchment and press down to flatten the avocado halves like slices of bologna.

Lightly spread the garlic cream across each slice of toast. It'll melt into the bread; that's good. Arrange the avocado bologna on top, then add a tangle of pickled carrots, using your fingers to lift the carrots and create lots of height. (We like to call these "salad fingers.") Garnish with the scallion and spice mix. Squeeze a little lemon juice over everything and finish with a sprinkle of fleur de sel.

NOTE ON GARLIC CREAM

You'll end up with more garlic cream than you need for two servings of toast, but this stuff is good on a lot of things. We once whipped it for too long and it turned into garlic butter—that was seriously good. Then we took that garlic butter, spread it on toasted bread, and rubbed a smashed tomato across the toast. Eating that dish will transport you to Spain in two seconds.

VEGAN OPTION

We get a lot of requests to make this dish vegan. All you have to do is leave out the garlic cream and brush the toast with olive oil instead of butter.

Pickled carrots

If you find beautiful thin carrots at the market, you can cut them on the bias into big pieces or even pickle them whole. They make great snacks.

Makes about 1 quart (1 L)

4 carrots (1 pound/455 g total)
2 or 3 sprigs fresh dill
2 or 3 sprigs fresh cilantro
1¼ cups (300 ml) distilled white or apple
   cider vinegar
1 dried red chile
¼ cup (50 g) sugar
1½ tablespoons coarse sea salt or kosher salt
½ teaspoon whole black peppercorns
6 cardamom pods
½ teaspoon coriander seeds
2 cloves garlic, crushed

Peel the carrots, then slice them lengthwise as thinly as possible. (We use the meat slicer, but you can use a mandoline or even just a vegetable peeler to get them paper-thin.) Place the sliced carrots in a 1-quart (1-L) jar or other container of a similar size. They should all fit, assuming you're leaving out the randomly shaped end pieces that you held on to while slicing. Stuff the dill and cilantro into the jar as well.

In a pot, combine the vinegar, chile, sugar, salt, peppercorns, cardamom, coriander, garlic, and 1 cup (240 ml) water. Heat, stirring to dissolve the sugar and salt. Remove from the heat, then pour over the sliced carrots. Cover and let sit at room temperature overnight.

Taste a pickled carrot and see if you like how pickled it is. Depending on how thinly you sliced the carrots, they could be pickled to your liking at this point. If they are not, move the jar to the refrigerator and let the carrots pickle for another day or two. Pickled carrots will keep in the fridge for at least 1 month.

Hass avocados at Schaner Family Farms in Valley Center, CA

Robin Koda, Koda Farms

"The land is really particular. We can't grow citrus because we're in this microclimate where it gets too cold and kills citrus. Whereas three miles down the road, it's growing in the street. But you know what we can grow. Rice."

Tuesday, February 23rd at 7:30 am. Robin Koda in conversation with Jessica Koslow

The spotlight follows Busy Philipps

Grains
& Beans
54—79

For every single rice dish we make at Sqirl, we use Kokuho Rose brown rice from Koda Farms. It is a medium-grain rice, unparalleled in quality, with a complex yet delicate flavor. There is a certain sweetness to it, and it works well both in sweet dishes (such as the Brown Rice Porridge) and also in savory dishes. Since the 1950s, the Koda family has been producing Kokuho Rose using time-honored techniques, organic growing practices, and never any GMOs. We're also committed to cooking with the cover crops grown during the off-season at Koda, and we've come up with a "cover crop stew," made with either garbanzo beans or black-eyed peas and usually some leafy greens.

Brown rice porridge

This is one of our OG dishes. We opened Sqirl during "winter" in California, when the temperature hovers around 65°F (18°C) and people tend to want something a little warmer for breakfast. It's similar to the Danish dish *risengrød*, which is traditionally served with butter and cinnamon. Our kitchen crew actually loves to eat this porridge cold. My go-to is the vegan variation of this porridge, served warm, with granola on top, plus a friendly dollop of jam.

Makes about 4 cups (960 ml); serves 4 (V, VVO)

1 cup (200 g) medium-grain brown rice
4 cups (960 ml) whole milk
¼ cup (50 g) sugar
½ teaspoon fine sea salt

½ vanilla bean
Chopped raw hazelnuts
Your favorite jam

Brown rice porridge

Rinse the rice in a fine-mesh sieve under cool water until the water runs clear. Transfer the rice to a large, heavy-bottomed pot. Pour in the milk and 4 cups (960 ml) water. Add the sugar and salt and stir to dissolve. Slice the ½ vanilla bean in half lengthwise and use the dull edge of your knife to scrape all the tiny black seeds into the pot. Drop in the scraped bean pod as well.

Bring to a boil. Watch the pot for the first few minutes; you want the liquid to boil but not boil over. Cook, stirring occasionally, until the rice is soft, the porridge is thick, and most of the liquid has evaporated, 60 to 70 minutes. At first it will seem like way too much liquid for so little rice, but with time it will evaporate. As the porridge gets closer and closer to being done, you'll need to stir more often to prevent the rice from sticking to the bottom of the pot.

Before serving, fish out and discard the vanilla bean pod. Top each bowl of porridge with a handful of hazelnuts and a spoonful of jam.

You can serve this porridge hot or cold, depending on what sounds best to you. When you chill it in the fridge, a skin will form on top. Don't be afraid of that. If you need to reheat it and it's a little too thick, add a splash of milk.

VEGAN VARIATION
Do not rinse the rice; the starch adds body. Use water in place of the milk. We always serve vegan brown rice porridge hot and we always add a splash of almond milk to the porridge while it heats up.

Buckwheat pancake with cocoa nib pudding

Sometimes we set this pancake in front of kids and they start bawling. That is not maple syrup on top! There are really two options here: (1) You can cook this pancake as shown in a little cast-iron skillet and top it with pudding, fruit, and sugar. That would be the "adult" version. (2) You can make the very same pancake batter, but cook individual silver dollar–size pancakes on a griddle or in a large pan. Stack them on a plate and serve a whole bowl of pudding and maple syrup on the side. That's the "cool dad" version.

Makes about 18 (3-inch/7.5-cm) silver dollar–size pancakes; serves 4 to 6 (GF, V)

FOR THE PUDDING

2½ cups (600 ml) almond milk (page 264 or store-bought)

3 tablespoons (25 g) cornstarch

⅓ cup (50 g) unsweetened cocoa powder

⅔ cup (140 g) granulated sugar

¼ teaspoon fine sea salt

1½ ounces (45 g) 70% chocolate, finely chopped

1½ teaspoons vanilla extract

½ cup (65 g) cocoa nibs

FOR THE PANCAKES

¾ cup (90 g) buckwheat flour, sifted

1 tablespoon cactus flour, sifted **(see Note)**

⅔ cup (80 g) corn flour (masa harina), sifted

¼ cup (55 g) packed brown sugar

1 teaspoon baking powder

½ teaspoon baking soda

¾ teaspoon fine sea salt

2 cups (480 ml) buttermilk

2 large eggs

6 tablespoons (90 g) unsalted butter, melted, plus more for the pan

Fresh fruit (such as persimmons and pomegranate in fall; blood orange segments in late winter; strawberries in spring; plum wedges in summer)

Confectioners' sugar

MAKE THE PUDDING

Pour ¼ cup (60 ml) of the almond milk into a small bowl and use a fork to stir in the cornstarch.

In a large, heavy-bottomed pot, whisk together the cocoa powder, sugar, and salt. While whisking slowly but continuously, pour in the remaining 2¼ cups (540 ml) almond milk. (This will help prevent clumps.) Bring to a gentle sim-mer over medium heat. Once the milk mixture bubbles, whisk in the cornstarch slurry. Continue cooking and whisking the pudding for a few minutes, until thick and smooth. The big, glossy bubbles should wink lazily at you.

Remove from the heat, then add the chocolate and vanilla, and keep whisking until the chocolate has melted into the pudding.

Transfer to a bowl and immediately lay a piece of plastic wrap directly on the surface of the pudding to prevent a skin from forming (unless you like pudding skin). The pudding can be made a couple of days ahead of time and stored in the fridge.

MAKE THE PANCAKES

In a large bowl, combine the buck-wheat flour, cactus flour, corn flour, brown sugar, baking powder,

Buckwheat pancake with cocoa nib pudding

baking soda, and salt. In another bowl, whisk together the buttermilk and eggs until airy and light yellow, about 3 minutes. (Use an electric mixer to make your life easier.) Pour the buttermilk-egg mixture into the flour mixture and whisk just until combined, then gradually whisk in the melted butter.

TO COOK INDIVIDUAL PANCAKES

Spoon the pancake batter onto a preheated griddle or large pan, adding a pat of butter to the pan before batches as needed to prevent sticking. Cook until the undersides of the pancakes are brown, then flip and cook until done.

ALTERNATIVELY, TO COOK LARGE PANCAKES

Preheat the oven to 350°F (175°C). Set four (6-inch/15-cm or smaller) cast-iron skillets over medium heat. Swirl about 1 tablespoon of butter into each skillet, then pour in enough batter to fill each skillet halfway. Cook for 1 minute, then transfer to the preheated oven and bake until cooked through, about 10 to 12 minutes.

SERVE THEM UP

Just before serving, stir the cocoa nibs into the pudding (they'll get soft if you leave them in there overnight or longer—which is fine, totally fine, I mean it's fine… it's just not the texture I'm after). Serve each stack of pancakes or each large pancake with a big dollop of pudding spread across one side of the top to make it look like a black-and-white cookie. Arrange the fruit in a line down the middle. Shower the confectioners' sugar over the other side.

CAN'T FIND CACTUS FLOUR?

Go online. Just kidding, don't worry too much—if you can't find it, add another 1 tablespoon corn flour to the pancake mix. The cactus flour adds acidity and lightness.

NOTE ON PUDDING

The vegan pudding by itself is fantastic. You could put it in a jar and serve it for dessert, adding as many cocoa nibs as you want for crunch.

FEEL LIKE WAFFLES INSTEAD?

This pancake batter works well in a waffle iron.

And then he made us pancakes…

Getting deep with Clancy Chassay and Milana Vayntrub

Sorrel pesto rice bowl

Sorrel pesto rice bowl

Kokuho Rose brown rice, nut-free sorrel pesto, preserved Meyer lemon, feta, and a poached egg

If I took this dish off the menu, I'm pretty sure we'd close. It has become the most iconic dish at Sqirl, even though you probably don't think of sorrel and preserved lemons as obvious breakfast foods. This dish succeeding is like when the horse that no one bet on ends up winning the Kentucky Derby. At first nobody even knew it was in the race. Then, all of a sudden, the long shot is ahead by leaps and bounds, and even its trainer looks confused.

Serves 6 (VO, VVO)

3 cups (600 g) medium-grain brown rice, preferably Kokuho Rose
Fine sea salt
½ cup plus 2 teaspoons (130 ml) extra-virgin olive oil
1 cup (25 g) lightly packed kale leaves (stems removed)
2 cups (50 g) lightly packed chopped sorrel leaves
3 tablespoons fresh lemon juice
2 tablespoons chopped fresh dill, plus more for serving

1 Preserved Meyer Lemon (recipe follows or store-bought), flesh removed, peel finely chopped
2 to 4 small watermelon radishes, very thinly sliced
¼ cup (60 ml) Fermented Jalapeño Hot Sauce (page 267)
¾ cup (85 g) crumbled sheep's-milk feta
6 poached eggs (page 22)
Fleur de sel
Freshly ground black pepper

Boil the rice in plenty of salted water until it's tender, 30 to 45 minutes. Drain and let cool.

Meanwhile, make the sorrel pesto: In a blender or food processor, combine ½ cup (120 ml) of the oil, kale, sorrel, and 1 tablespoon of the lemon juice. Blend until smooth, stopping and scraping down the sides as needed. Season with salt to taste.

In a large bowl, toss the rice with the dill, preserved lemon peel, 1 tablespoon of the lemon juice, and the pesto. Taste and add a bit more salt, if needed.

In a small bowl, toss the radish with the remaining 1 tablespoon lemon juice, the remaining 2 teaspoons oil, and a pinch of salt. Set aside to marinate for a few minutes, until the radish is pliable and tender.

To serve, divide the rice among six bowls. Spoon a line of hot sauce across the rice. Arrange a little clump of feta on one side and a rosette of radish slices on the other side. Set a poached egg in the middle of each bowl and season it with fleur de sel and black pepper. Garnish with a tiny sprig or two of dill.

MAKE IT YOURS

Think of this rice bowl as a solid base for you to build upon. Don't like poached eggs? Leave them out. Make it a Meat Lovers' by adding bacon (page 115) and breakfast sausage (page 117). Or go the vegan route and substitute kale for the feta and eggs. We like to toss the kale in our Southern-Style Fresh Cream and Black Mustard Dressing (page 266) before adding it to the bowl.

Preserved Meyer lemons

Meyer lemons
Fine sea salt or Diamond Crystal kosher salt, as needed

Sorrel pesto rice bowl

With one hand, hold a lemon stem-side down on a cutting board. With the other hand (and a knife), cut down through the middle of the lemon, stopping when you have almost reached the stem. Rotate the lemon 90 degrees and cut down through the middle once again, creating a cross-shaped cut. You should now have a lemon that is held together at the stem end and that flowers open into four quarters on the blossom end.

Hold the cut lemon over a bowl. Pull it open and stuff in a really big pinch (about 1 tablespoon) of salt. Continue stuffing the cut lemons with salt, picking up and reusing any salt that falls into the bowl.

Turn each lemon upside down so that the cut end is pointed straight down to the bowl, and press the lemon against the bottom of the bowl to make it splay open. It's okay if the quarters break apart. Put the flattened lemon into a crock or a nonreactive container such as a jar, and press down to compress it. Add more lemons as needed to fill the container.

If you're using a crock, set a ceramic weight or plate on top of the lemons to weigh them down. If you're using a jar or some other container, you'll need to fill a plastic bag with a brine made of 2 cups (480 ml) water and ¼ cup (35 g) salt. Get as much air out of the bag as possible, then seal it well. Pack the bag weight into the jar on top of the lemons, sealing the salted lemons from the air. Instead of using a bag weight, you could use a smaller jar that fits inside and weighs down the salted lemons. Cover with cheesecloth and secure it with a rubber band.

Label and date the jar, then let it sit in a dark, cool spot, covered, for about 2 weeks. During summer, it only takes about 10 days, but during winter, it sometimes takes 4 weeks. You'll know the lemons are done preserving when the white pith is not white anymore; it will be translucent.

Once they are preserved, they will keep in the refrigerator for months.

To use the preserved lemons, discard any seeds, scrape off the juicy flesh part (and save for making salad dressing), and use only the rind.

NOTE
During the first few hours, the lemons should release enough liquid to stay fully submerged. If they don't, dissolve 2 tablespoons salt in 1 cup (240 ml) water and pour in enough of this brine to cover.

Isaac and Elie Resnikoff, right before they were beamed into outer space

Crispy rice salad

Kokuho Rose fried brown rice, lemongrass, mint, cucumber, and ginger

This is a riff on *nam khao*, a rice salad from Laos. Night + Market restaurant in LA makes a great version with funky sour sausage, and you should definitely go there if you're looking for the traditional dish.

Serves 2 (VO, VVO)

1 cup (200 g) medium-grain brown rice
Non-GMO canola oil (for frying; about 4 cups/960 ml)
Fine sea salt and freshly ground black pepper
2-inch (5-cm) knob of ginger, cut in half
¼ cup (60 ml) fresh lemon juice

2 small Persian cucumbers, very thinly sliced
¼ cup (13 g) fresh mint leaves, chopped
¼ cup (13 g) fresh cilantro leaves, chopped
2 scallions, thinly sliced on the bias
2 to 3 tablespoons hot sauce (page 267 or store-bought)

THE NIGHT BEFORE YOU PLAN TO SERVE THE CRISPY RICE SALAD

Cook the rice by boiling it in plenty of water until tender, about 30 minutes or so. While it cooks, stir a few times so it doesn't stick to the pot. Drain in a fine-mesh sieve and let it really drip for a good 5 to 10 minutes, then spread it out on a towel-lined plate and place in the refrigerator, uncovered, to dry overnight.

ON THE FOLLOWING DAY

Pour at least 3 inches (7.5 cm) of oil into a wide pot and heat the oil to 350°F (175°C). Carefully drop the rice into the hot oil all at once—it's going to bubble feverishly, so stand back from the stove for a few seconds and then come back when you hear it subside. Do not stir the rice; it will stick. After a minute or two, the rice will look golden. At this point, you can use a slotted spoon or wire spider to stir. Once the rice is crisp, transfer it to a plate lined with a brown paper bag, season with salt and pepper, and let cool.

NEXT, MAKE AN INFUSED LEMON JUICE

Combine the ginger and lemon juice in a small bowl. Let the lemon juice infuse for at least 30 minutes.

Transfer the crispy rice to a large bowl. Run your fingers through it to break up any big clumps. Add the cucumber, mint, cilantro, and scallions. Pour in 1 tablespoon of the infused lemon juice, leaving the ginger behind, and 2 tablespoons hot sauce. Taste and add more infused lemon juice or hot sauce (or both), depending on how acidic and how spicy you want the rice to be. Add a pinch of salt and toss well. Serve in one of the following ways:

FRIED EGG ON TOP

The best time to fry the eggs (see page 22) is after you've combined the crispy rice with the cucumber and herbs but before you add the infused lemon juice and hot sauce.

"THE WORKS"

Lots of people like to order this salad topped with both a fried egg and house-made breakfast sausage (page 117). For the sausage, we cook the patty a bit, then we chop it up and add it back to the pan, where it cooks further and gets crisp, brown, and delicious. Mix it into the rice before serving.

THE CRISPY VEGAN

Serve each portion of this salad by first putting a handful of small, leafy mixed lettuces into the bowl. Then, add the rice and place ½ avocado, sliced, on top. (We always season avocado with fleur de sel, pepper, and a little lemon juice.) To throw you for a loop, people love to order a "crispy vegan with the works."

Chickpea stew with chard, poached eggs, and smoked chilie

Chickpea stew with chard, poached eggs, and smoked chile

Aioli adds a luxurious texture without being heavy cream. But if you don't want to add it, don't worry about it—the stew is great on its own.

Serves 6 (V)

1 cup (180 g) dried garbanzo beans
Fine sea salt
3 tablespoons extra-virgin olive oil
1 small yellow onion, diced
2 cloves garlic, thinly sliced
½-inch (12-mm) knob of ginger, peeled and finely grated
Pinch of ground cinnamon
1 teaspoon smoked chile powder
3 canned tomatoes, coarsely chopped

TO SERVE

6 poached eggs (page 22)
2 big handfuls (about 60 g) very thinly sliced chard leaves
½ lemon
½ cup (115 g) aioli (page 263; optional)
Baguette toast

In a large bowl, combine the garbanzos, 1½ teaspoons salt, and enough lukewarm water to cover by a few inches. Let soak at room temperature overnight.

On the following day, drain and rinse the garbanzos and put them in a pot. Add 2 teaspoons salt and 4 cups (960 ml) fresh water. Bring to a boil, then reduce the heat so the water simmers gently. Cook until the garbanzos are tender and creamy all the way through and not chalky at all, 45 to 60 minutes. Add water as needed to keep the garbanzos submerged.

Transfer the garbanzos and their cooking liquid to a bowl.

Return the empty pot to the stove over medium heat. Add the oil, onion, and ¼ teaspoon salt. Cook, stirring occasionally, until the onion softens, about 2 minutes. Add the garlic, ginger, cinnamon, and chile powder. Let sizzle for a moment, then add the tomatoes. Cook for a few minutes, stirring and scraping the bottom of the pot only every so often. The tomato will stick to the pot and brown—that's good. Scrape it up and let it do that a few times. Add the garbanzos and their liquid. There may not be that much liquid, and if you want the beans to be really stewy, you could add another ½ cup (120 ml) water to the pot. Adjust the heat so that the liquid bubbles gently, then cook for

about 5 minutes, until the flavors have melded.

Using a slotted spoon, scoop out about half the garbanzos, smash them (with a potato masher or even some vigorous fork action), and then return them to the pot.

To serve, spoon the stew into bowls. Top each bowl with a poached egg, a tangle of chard, and a big squeeze of lemon juice. Dollop a spoonful of aioli on top, if you're using it, and enjoy with toast.

OKRA ADDITION

When okra is in season, we'll char some and confit some and add them both to this stew.

The sprouty pod

Mung bean sprouts, crunchy buckwheat, and roasted delicata squash with pomegranate, labneh, and cilantro pistou

We used to think of the grain bowl as a go-to dish, but now we find ourselves asking, how can we add more sprouts to our diet? Here's one way.

Serves 6 as a light lunch or a first course (V, VVO)

FOR THE MUNG BEAN SPROUTS

¼ cup (45 g) dried mung beans

FOR THE LABNEH (see Note)

1 cup (240 g) plain whole-milk yogurt
Fine sea salt

FOR THE CRUNCHY BUCKWHEAT

½ cup (80 g) hulled buckwheat groats

FOR THE ROASTED DELICATA SQUASH

2 large or 3 small delicata squash
    (3 pounds/1.4 kg total)
3 tablespoons extra-virgin olive oil, plus more
    for drizzling
½ teaspoon ground coriander
Fine sea salt and freshly ground black pepper

FOR THE CILANTRO PISTOU

1 clove garlic
2 tablespoons fresh lemon juice
¼ teaspoon fine sea salt
½ bunch cilantro
⅓ cup (80 ml) extra-virgin olive oil

TO SERVE

1 cup (180 g) pomegranate arils
½ bunch cilantro
Really good olive oil
2 limes, halved
Fleur de sel

MAKE THE SPROUTS

(Don't feel like making sprouts? I get you. Go to the store and buy a couple of clamshells, then skip ahead to the labneh.) Place the mung beans in a 1-quart (1-L) jar, add plenty of water to cover, and let soak for at least 8 hours at room temperature.

Pour off almost all the water, leaving the soaked beans in the jar. Cover the jar with a piece of cheesecloth and secure it with a rubber band. Invert the jar and prop the bottom of it up so that the residual water can drain out. We set this up using the edge of a rimmed baking sheet. You could lean the jar against the inside of a pie dish, or you could invent any kind of setup that works well in your kitchen. The idea here is to keep the beans hydrated but not soaked and also to expose them to lots of air so they will sprout. Or, I guess, you could just keep the cheesecloth-covered jar upright, but that's not nearly as fun.

About every 12 hours, fill the jar with water, gently swirl it around to rinse the beans, then pour out the water and prop the jar up again. After 24 hours or so, almost all the beans will have sprouted little tails. Once the sprouts are ⅜ inch (1 cm) long (or however long you'd like them to be), cover the jar and transfer to the fridge, where the sprouts will continue to grow a tiny bit.

MAKE THE LABNEH

(Don't feel like making labneh? Go to a Middle Eastern grocery store and buy a cup, then skip ahead to the crunchy buckwheat.) Line the inside of a colander with a double layer of cheesecloth and place the colander inside a larger bowl. The bottom of the colander shouldn't touch the bottom of the bowl—you want it to hover. Spoon the yogurt into the colander and let it drain in the fridge for 8 to 24 hours, depending on how thick you'd like it to be. Obviously, the longer it drains, the thicker it'll get. For this recipe, I like it to be pretty thick, almost a paste.

Once the labneh is your desired consistency, transfer it to a bowl and season with salt. Transfer to a container and keep in the refrigerator for up to 1 month. (Keep the whey that has dripped through the cheesecloth and use it for things like cooking vegetables [page 77], kick-starting lactofermented pickles, flavoring soups, or even fertilizing. Grow a rosemary bush!)

MAKE THE CRUNCHY BUCKWHEAT

Preheat the oven to 350°F (175°C).

Spread the buckwheat out on a dry, rimmed baking sheet. Toast in the oven until golden brown and crunchy, about 10 minutes.

MAKE THE ROASTED DELICATA SQUASH

Adjust the oven temperature to 425°F (220°C).

Cut the squash in half lengthwise. Scoop out and discard the seeds, but do not peel the skin—it's tender and delicious. Cut the squash into 2- to 3-inch (5- to 7.5-cm) chunks and set on a rimmed baking sheet. Toss with just enough oil to barely coat, about 3 tablespoons. Sprinkle the coriander evenly over the squash pieces. Season lightly with salt and a few grinds of pepper. Bake until tender all the way through and a little caramelized on the bottom, 30 to 40 minutes. Let cool.

MAKE THE CILANTRO PISTOU

In a blender, combine the garlic, lemon juice, and salt. Blend on low speed until the garlic is finely chopped and mostly incorporated into the lemon juice. Cut the sprigs of cilantro right at the point where the leaves start branching from the stems. Take the leafy top part and drop it into the blender. Blend on the lowest speed until the cilantro is coarsely chopped and there are still big pieces of leaves, about 10 seconds. Gradually increase the speed while you slowly pour in the oil. Once you've added all the oil, blend on high speed for 20 seconds. The pistou will be emulsified and flecked with green cilantro leaves. (You can also make it by hand, first chopping the garlic and herbs, then whisking the lemon juice and oil together.)

TO SERVE

Schmear 1 to 2 tablespoons of the labneh in the bottom of each bowl. Scatter a small handful of sprouts and pomegranate seeds over the labneh, then drizzle with 1 to 2 tablespoons of the pistou. Top with a few pieces of squash, more sprouts and pomegranate seeds, and a spoonful of crunchy buckwheat. Sprinkle some cilantro leaves over everything. Finish with a drizzle of oil, a final spoonful of pistou, a strong squeeze of lime juice, and a pinch of fleur de sel.

NOTE ON LABNEH

After 24 hours of straining through cheesecloth, most yogurts will have lost about half their volume. If you find out that you like labneh, make a double batch and use it on all kinds of dishes. We tend to add a dollop when a dish is begging for a creamy element.

NOTE ON MAKING THIS VEGAN

Leave out the labneh.

The sprouty pod

Shin Okuda going places. But, first, breakfast.

Sprouted lentil soup with green garlic puree

Sprouted lentil soup with green garlic puree

Stirring a bright green puree (made of fresh herbs or blanched greens) into soup just before serving is a trick restaurants use to bring intense color to a dish. For this sprouted lentil soup, we use a green garlic puree. It will add some serious panache to your meal.

Makes 4 cups (960 ml); serves 4 (VV)

1 cup (200 g) dried le Puy green lentils
Fine sea salt
3 tablespoons extra-virgin olive oil
1 cup (130 g) finely chopped shallot
   (about 3 large)
½ cup (60 g) finely chopped fennel
   (about ½ small)
½ cup (60 g) finely chopped parsnip
   (about 1 small)

½ cup (60 g) finely chopped celery
   (about 2 stalks)
1 cup (55 g) thinly sliced green garlic
1 cup (55 g) kohlrabi greens or spinach,
   stems removed
½ lemon
Sprouting broccoli flowers (optional)
¼ cup (13 g) chopped dill

First, decide if you want to sprout the lentils. I like sprouting them because they cook down really quickly. If you choose yes, follow the technique for mung bean sprouts on page 71. If you choose no, put the lentils in a bowl, pour boiling water over them to cover, and let soak for 10 minutes. Drain well.

In a large pot, combine the lentils, 3 cups (720 ml) fresh water, and ¾ teaspoon salt. Simmer gently until the lentils are completely tender, 10 to 20 minutes, depending on if they were sprouted or not.

Meanwhile, heat a large pan over medium heat and add the oil, shallot, fennel, parsnip, celery, and ¾ tea-spoon salt. Cook, stirring often, until the vegetables are soft but not yet browned, about 5 minutes.

Stir the vegetables into the cooked lentils, remove from the heat, and let the two meld together while you prepare the green garlic puree.

Bring a small pot (last one, promise!) of salted water to a boil. Drop the green garlic into the boiling water and cook for 30 seconds, until tender and bright green. Using a slotted spoon, transfer the green garlic to a plate and place it in the freezer to cool. Puree in a mini food processor, adding as little cold water as needed to get the garlic spinning. Alternatively, use a large knife to chop the garlic as finely as possible. You won't get as smooth a puree this way, but it has the added benefit of dirtying one less kitchen appliance. (Green garlic puree can hang out, covered, in the fridge for a couple of days, until it loses its vibrant color.)

To serve, heat the lentil soup to a boil. Stir in the kohlrabi greens and let them wilt. Taste and adjust the seasoning, adding salt as needed. Stir in the green garlic puree—this will turn the soup bright green. Add a generous squeeze of lemon juice, and ladle into bowls. Garnish with flowers and dill.

Seared polenta cake with seasonal vegetable medley

Seared polenta cake with seasonal vegetable medley

A lot of people come to Sqirl looking to order a gluten-free dish. Something warm, vegetable heavy, and maybe not a hash. Our seared polenta cake hits all those marks.

For the vegetable medley, use your favorites. During spring, this could be English peas and/or whole snap peas, 1-inch (2.5-cm) segments of asparagus, pea tendrils, snipped fresh chives, and sliced scallions; during summer and fall, try cauliflower florets, carrots sliced on the bias, thin slices of summer squash, and fresh opal basil.

Serves 6 to 8 (V)

FOR THE POLENTA CAKES

1 cup (240 ml) milk
2 cups (280 g) coarse polenta
Fine sea salt
7 tablespoons (100 g) unsalted butter, plus
   more for the baking dish

FOR THE VEGETABLE MEDLEY

4 tablespoons (85 g) unsalted butter
½ cup (65 g) finely chopped red onion
Fine sea salt

4 cups (540 g) chopped vegetables of your choosing
¾ cup (180 ml) whey from making ricotta (page
   268) or labneh (page 71)
½ lemon

TO SERVE

1 tablespoon chopped fresh chives
3 tablespoons thinly sliced fresh basil leaves
Fine sea salt
Fried eggs (page 22; optional)

MAKE THE POLENTA CAKES

Bring the milk and 5 cups (1.2 L) water to a boil in a large, heavy-bottomed pot. While whisking continuously, gradually add the polenta. Don't stop whisking until the polenta begins to absorb some of the liquid. At first it'll just sink to the bottom of the pot, but then it will float and combine. Add 1 teaspoon salt. Reduce the heat to low so the polenta bubbles gently. Cook, stirring occasionally with a long-handled spoon to avoid splatters and burns, until the polenta tastes tender and no longer crunchy, 20 to 30 minutes. Remove from the heat, then stir in 5 tablespoons (70 g) of the butter. Once the butter has melted, taste the polenta, adding more salt, if needed.

Butter an 8-inch (20-cm) square baking dish. Pour the polenta into the dish, smooth it out, and let cool until firm.

Once the polenta is completely cool, cut it into 6 to 8 rectangles. It's just like cutting brownies, but these are bigger.

Next, set two skillets on the stove. You're going to sear the polenta in one skillet and cook the vegetable medley in the other at the same time.

START WITH THE MEDLEY

Heat one skillet over medium-high heat and add in 2 tablespoons butter. Add the onion and a pinch of salt, and cook until the onion turns translucent, 4 to 5 minutes. Add the vegetables and ¼ teaspoon salt and cook, stirring often, until the vegetables soften a little, 1 to 2 minutes, depending on what kind of vegetables you're using. When they're a little soft, add the whey. Let it really bubble for a couple of minutes.

Meanwhile, melt 2 tablespoons butter in the second skillet over high heat, then add the polenta cakes, arranging them so they fit in a single layer. Sear for 2 to 4 minutes, then flip and remove the pan from the heat.

Once most of the whey has evaporated, add the remaining 2 tablespoons butter and a big squeeze of lemon juice to the vegetables. Stir to incorporate the butter, then remove from the heat.

Set a polenta cake, seared-side up, in the center of each plate. Spoon some of the vegetable medley over the top. Finish with a sprinkling of the chives and basil and another squeeze of lemon juice. Serve topped with a fried egg, if you like.

Seared polenta cake with seasonal vegetable medley

James Birch of Flora Bella Farm

"So I went into the mountains. I have deer, I have gophers. I said, you know, there're all these animals here and I'm creating this salad bar. And I'm willing to share it with them, as long as they only take 20 percent and I get 80 percent. And once it goes over that, well, in the old days I would probably think about shooting them. But I won't hurt any animals today. I'll build a fence."

Saturday, March 5th at 3 pm. James Birch in conversation with Jessica Koslow

Louie Wasserman, making a spectacle of himself

Vege-tables
82–109

I don't know whether or not to be proud of this, but I've become known for making dishes that appear simple at first glance but actually involve a lot of steps to get there. It can be rewarding to go through all those steps and end up with a final dish that has many layers of flavor. But it's also rewarding and possible to cook something delicious in less than an hour and have it done in time for dinner. So, throughout this book, and especially in this chapter, I'll point out where you can use store-bought ingredients and where you can skip over steps if you're in a hurry. There are always ways you can modify these recipes to suit your own tastes and time constraints.

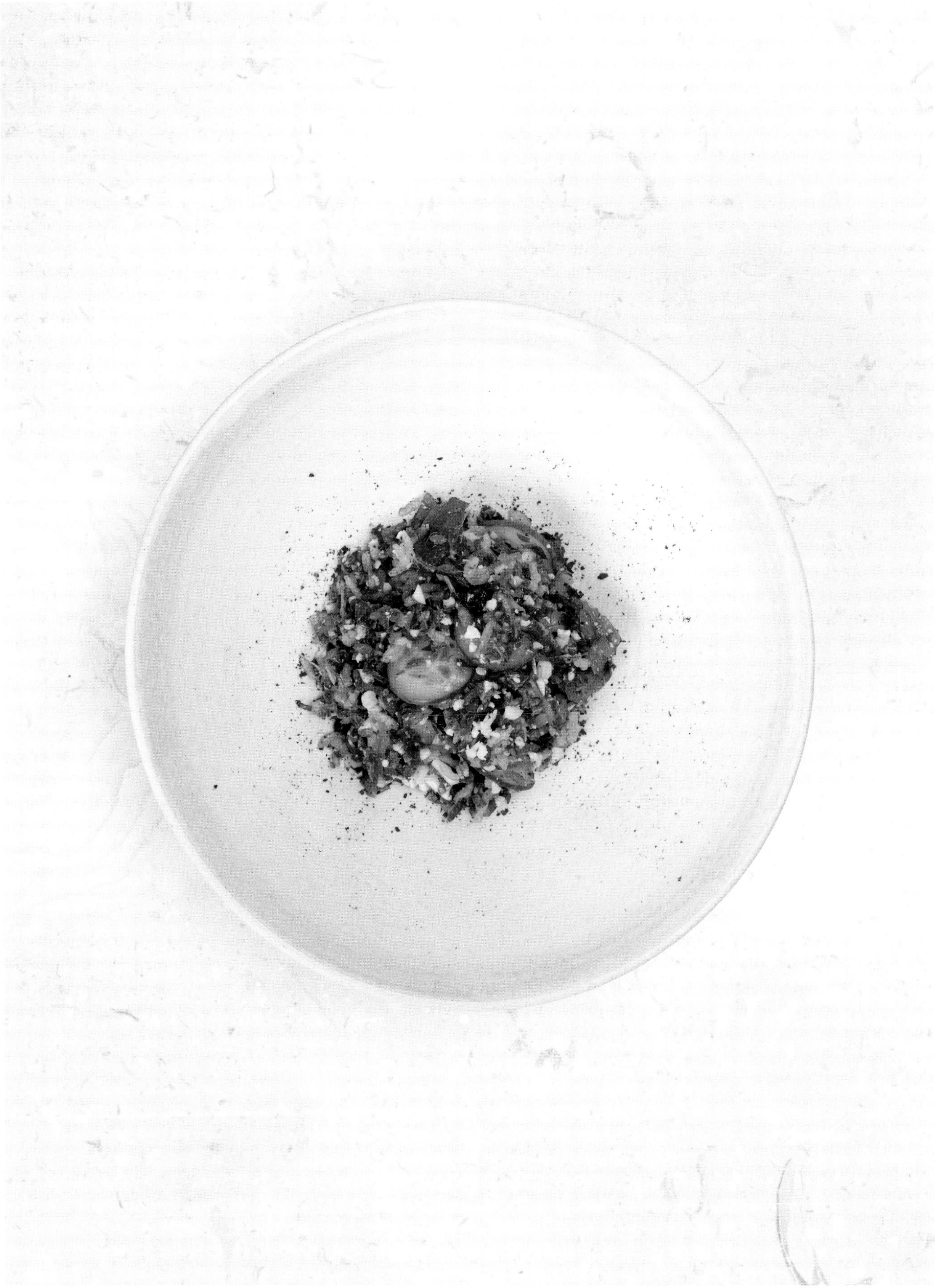

Kabbouleh

Kabbouleh

If you don't have sumac and Aleppo pepper, don't let that stop you from making this dish. It will still be delicious.

Serves 4 (VV)

½ cup (100 g) medium-grain brown rice
Non-GMO canola oil (for frying; about 4 cups/960 ml)
Fine sea salt and freshly ground black pepper
¼ cup (60 ml) red wine vinegar
1 teaspoon fresh thyme leaves
1 clove garlic, smashed
1½ teaspoons sugar
¼ cup (35 g) dried currants
⅓ cup (80 ml) extra-virgin olive oil

1 tablespoon ground sumac
1 teaspoon ground Aleppo pepper or urfa biber or dried chile flakes
1½ cups (200 g) coarsely chopped cauliflower florets
1 small bunch (220 g) green kale, ribs and stems removed
1 scallion, very thinly sliced on the bias
1 Persian cucumber, very thinly sliced crosswise

Follow the instructions on page 66 for boiling, drying, and frying the rice. For this recipe, you'll need only ½ cup (100 g) of rice to begin with, but it will cook in the same amount of time as described on page 66.

In a small pot, combine the vinegar, thyme, garlic, sugar, currants, and ¼ teaspoon salt. Bring to a boil, then remove from the heat and let the currants get plump in the hot vinegar. Once the vinegar has cooled off, strain it into a small bowl and save the currants for adding later on. Whisk the olive oil into the vinegar, then whisk in the sumac and Aleppo. Taste for seasoning, adding another pinch of sugar or salt if needed. It should taste quite tart.

In the bowl of a food processor fitted with a metal blade, whiz the cauliflower until finely chopped,

then transfer to a large bowl. Put the kale in the bowl of the food processor and pulse until finely chopped. Add the kale to the bowl with the cauliflower. Mix in the scallion, cucumber, crispy rice, and soaked currants, and pour in some of the dressing. Mix well and taste, adding more dressing and another pinch of salt, if you like. Serve immediately.

If you want to make this ahead, combine everything except the crispy rice—you want it to stay crispy. Mix it in just before serving.

NOTE ON THE NAME

I'm not the biggest fan of tomatoes in tabbouleh. I like them at the peak of summer, but what about when you want to eat tabbouleh in January? This is my winter version, true to the ingredients that are available during the cold months.

VARIATION

Add ½ cup (90 g) pomegranate arils when they're in season.

ALTERNATIVES TO FRYING THE RICE

I've heard of people using Indian puffed rice cereal instead of the crispy fried rice. We tested it and it's good! It doesn't give that same crunch, though, so it's best to eat it right away. You could also consider using dehydrated quinoa (page 165).

NOTE ON THE FRYING OIL

Don't throw out the oil. You can definitely reuse it to fry a second time or use it in another recipe that calls for canola oil.

Crunchy sprout salad with kohlrabi, beet, and herby crème fraîche dressing

Are you a sailor suffering from scurvy on a voyage in the 1700s? Or are you just a person reading this book, looking for a salad to make? Either way, you need more sprouts in your life. And if you're looking for even more, try the Sprouty Pod (page 71) or the Sprouted Lentil Soup (page 75).

Serves 6 (V, VVO)

Fine sea salt

6 small beets (14 ounces/400 g total), scrubbed

1 bunch fresh cilantro, tough bottom stems trimmed

½ bunch fresh mint, tough bottom stems trimmed

1 bunch fresh flat-leaf parsley, tough bottom stems trimmed

2 teaspoons ground coriander seeds

1 cup (240 ml) crème fraîche (page 265 or store-bought)

4 large radishes (5 ounces/140 g total), cut into very thin wedges

2 small kohlrabi or 1 bulb fennel (14 ounces/400 g total), peeled and diced into ½-inch (12-mm) cubes

¼ cup (25 g) lentil sprouts

¼ cup (25 g) mung bean sprouts

¼ cup (25 g) sunflower sprouts

2 lemons, halved

2 tablespoons extra-virgin olive oil

3 tablespoons sunflower seeds, toasted

Fleur de sel

Bring a large pot of salted water to a boil. Add the beets and cook until tender all the way through, 35 to 45 minutes.

While the beets boil, make the dressing: Bring another pot of salted water to a boil. Set a small handful of cilantro leaves aside, then add the remaining cilantro to the pot along with the mint and parsley. Cook the herbs for about 10 seconds.

Using tongs, transfer the herbs to a plate and pop the plate in the freezer for a few minutes. (This step is in lieu of shocking the herbs in an ice bath. Hey, we're low on water out here!)

Use your hands to squeeze out any excess water left clinging to the herbs. Puree the herbs using a food processor or a high-speed blender, adding only as much cool water as needed to get the herbs moving. The herb puree should be thick but pretty smooth. Stir it and the coriander into the crème fraîche. Season with salt and set aside.

Once the beets are done, drain and peel them, then cut into small wedges.

To serve, smear about half the herby crème fraîche across a large platter. Arrange the beet wedges, radishes, kohlrabi, and sprouts on top. Squeeze a good amount of lemon juice over everything and drizzle the olive oil over. Spoon the remaining dressing over the salad. Garnish with the reserved cilantro leaves, toasted sunflower seeds, and a few generous pinches of fleur de sel.

NOTE ON BEETS

We like to serve this salad with both cooked beets and fermented beets. If that idea appeals to you, here's how to make fermented beets: Stir ½ cup (65 g) kosher salt into 8 cups (2 L) water until dissolved. Add some spices (try 6 peppercorns, 10 coriander seeds, 20 dill seeds, and 3 smashed cloves garlic) and add 6 to 8 small raw beets. Weight down the beets so they are fully submerged. Cover with cheesecloth, secure with a rubber band, and leave out at room temperature for 7 to 10 days, until the beets taste sour and a little funky. Slice thinly and add to this dish (and others). Store any unused fermented beets in their liquid in the refrigerator for up to several months.

NEED PROTEIN?

Add smoked trout to this salad. When I was little, my mom and I would return from the market with a bag of mixed sprouts and I would toss them in a bowl with a can of tuna. I'd add lemon juice, olive oil, salt, and pepper and—voilà! Lunch was served with pride.

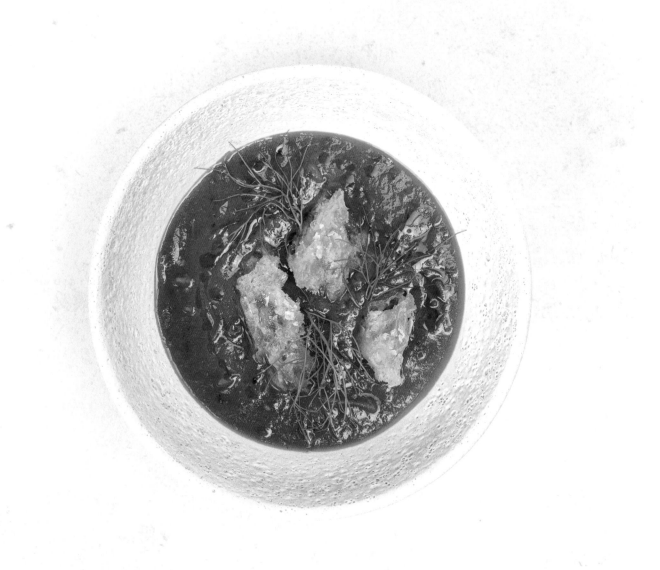

Charred tomato soup with mint and croutons

Charred tomato soup with mint and croutons

This clean, easy soup is perfect in the dead of summer. It's really delicious cold.

Makes about 4 cups (960 ml); serves 4 (VV, GFO)

½ baguette (about 150 g)
Extra-virgin olive oil
Fine sea salt
4 large red tomatoes (about 2 pounds/
    910 g total)

2 teaspoons sherry vinegar, plus more as
    needed
6 fresh mint leaves
Fleur de sel
Tiny fennel fronds (optional)

Preheat the oven to 350°F (175°C).

Cut the crust off the baguette. (The crust pieces can be toasted until completely dry and then ground to bread crumbs and saved for another use.) Tear the baguette into crouton-size pieces and spread them out on a rimmed baking sheet. Drizzle 3 tablespoons oil over the bread, then toss to coat, gently squeezing the bread so that it soaks up the oil. Season evenly with ¼ teaspoon salt. Bake, stirring once or twice, until golden brown and crisp on the outside but still chewy on the inside, about 15 minutes.

Use the tip of a small knife to cut out the stem end of the tomatoes, then slice the tomatoes in half through the equator.

Heat a large pan over high heat for 2 minutes. When the pan is ripping hot, add 2 tablespoons oil. Place as many tomato halves as will fit in a single layer in the pan, cut-side down. Sear until lightly charred in a few places, 3 to 6 minutes. Using tongs, transfer the charred tomatoes to a plate and put the next batch in the pan to sear. Add a little more oil before each batch goes in, if the pan looks dry.

Add the vinegar, mint leaves, and 1 teaspoon of salt into a blender letting the salt dissolve. Then scrape the tomatoes and any of their juices left behind in the pan into a blender. Blend on low speed, just to break up the tomatoes, then increase the speed to medium and, while blending, gradually pour in ½ cup (120 ml) oil. Blend on high speed for 1 minute.

Taste the soup and adjust the seasoning, adding more salt or vinegar, if it needs it.

Strain the soup through a nut-milk bag. (The strained seeds and pulp can be dehydrated until crisp and then turned into tomato powder— see page 99.)

Pour the soup into four bowls and top each with croutons, a drizzle of oil, and a sprinkle of fleur de sel. Garnish with fennel fronds.

LIKE A LITTLE TEXTURE IN YOUR SOUP?
Don't strain it.

NOTE ON SERVING
You can serve this soup hot or cold. It will taste even better the day after you make it.

Brussels sprouts two ways

Brussels sprouts two ways
Shaved raw and pan-roasted Brussels sprouts with roasted pears

A lot of chefs use the great trick of highlighting an ingredient by using it in two different ways within the same dish. If you're making a beet salad, you could emulsify some of the cooked beets and use them in the dressing. You can do this easily with both fruits and vegetables. In this recipe, I borrow that trickery and use it as a way to get more pear into the dish.

Serves 6 (V)

2 to 3 Warren pears (1 pound 5 ounces/600 g total **(see Note)**
6 tablespoons (85 g) unsalted butter
2 tablespoons champagne vinegar or white wine vinegar
1 teaspoon honey
Fine sea salt
½ cup (120 ml) extra-virgin olive oil

2 pounds 10 ounces (1.1 kg) Brussels sprouts, trimmed
1 tablespoon sherry vinegar
¾ cup (130 g) pomegranate arils (from ½ medium fruit)
⅓ cup (45 g) toasted chopped hazelnuts
¼ cup (13 g) lightly packed fresh flat-leaf parsley leaves, chopped, plus more for garnish
½ lemon

Cut the pears lengthwise into quarters, scoop out the cores, and trim off the stems.

Melt 2 tablespoons of the butter in a wide pan over medium-high heat. Add 1 pear (4 quarters), cut-sides down, to the pan and cook until lightly caramelized, about 2 minutes. Rotate and caramelize the other cut sides for another 1 to 2 minutes, until tender but not mushy.

Transfer to the bowl of a food processor fitted with a metal blade. Add the champagne vinegar, honey, and ½ teaspoon salt. Blend until completely pureed. Then, with the motor running, slowly drizzle in the oil and continue blending until the dressing is emulsified.

Cut 1 pound (455 g) of the Brussels sprouts in half. Doing so will cause some of the outermost leaves to fall off. Keep the loose leaves in a little pile on your cutting board.

Return the pan to the stove and heat over medium-high heat for 2 minutes. Add the remaining 4 table-spoons (60 g) butter. As soon as the foam subsides, add the cut Brussels to the pan, arranging each one cut-side down. (I know this seems like a pain, but it will ensure that the sprouts cook evenly.) Cook, without stirring the sprouts, for 2 to 3 minutes. Flip, season evenly with ½ teaspoon salt, and cook the rounded sides for another 2 minutes.

Add the reserved outer leaves and the sherry vinegar, and shake the pan to distribute. Cook for 10 more seconds, just to wilt the leaves, then transfer to a plate.

Shave the remaining raw Brussels sprouts thinly on a mandoline. (Fingers, be careful!) This takes forever with a knife, but a food processor fitted with a slicing/shredding blade would also work. Toss the shaved sprouts into a large bowl. Add the pomegranate seeds, hazelnuts, parsley, about three-quarters of the dressing, and ½ teaspoon salt. Toss to coat everything well. Taste, adding a bit more salt or dressing, if you want. Thinly slice the remaining pear quarters. Serve the salad with the pan-roasted Brussels and the sliced pears tucked in. Finish with a big squeeze of lemon juice, and a handful of parsley on top.

NOTE ON WARREN PEARS
Warrens are super sweet and have a velvety, grit-free texture like butter that gives this dressing great body. If you can't find any, use Red d'Anjou.

Socca (chickpea flour pancakes)

made with your choice of zucchini, carrot, or winter squash

Since Sqirl is open for breakfast and lunch, the majority of our customers order one dish, not an appetizer followed by an entrée and a cheese course. So we are always trying to come up with ways to create a single dish that really satisfies. This socca pancake stemmed from that quest. It's traditional in that it is a flat pancake made of gluten-free chickpea flour, but it's also not so traditional in that it is filled with lots of vegetables and topped with greens and creamy labneh.

Serves 4 (V, GF)

1 pound (455 g) zucchini, carrot, or winter squash **(see Notes)**, peeled and coarsely grated
Fine sea salt
¼ teaspoon cumin seeds
¼ teaspoon coriander seeds
¼ teaspoon fennel seeds
4 large eggs
1 clove garlic, minced
1 tablespoon chopped fresh oregano
2 tablespoons chopped fresh mint
3 tablespoons chopped fresh cilantro

⅔ cup (80 g) chickpea flour
Freshly ground black pepper
Pinch of ground cinnamon (optional; use with winter squash)
Pinch of ground ginger (optional; use with winter squash)
2 tablespoons unsalted butter, plus more as needed
½ cup (120 ml) labneh (page 71 or store-bought)
3 cups (60 g) spicy greens (such as watercress, arugula, or baby mustard greens)
1 tablespoon fresh lemon juice
1 tablespoon extra-virgin olive oil

Toss the grated vegetable with a few big pinches of salt, then put it in a fine-mesh sieve and let drain, squeezing every so often so that the vegetable releases its water, for at least 15 minutes.

Meanwhile, combine the cumin, coriander, and fennel seeds in a dry skillet over medium-low heat. Toast the spices, shaking the pan often, until fragrant but not burned, about 3 minutes. Using a mortar and pestle or a spice grinder, grind the toasted spices to a powder.

Crack the eggs into a large bowl and whisk to break them up. Add the drained vegetables, along with the garlic, oregano, mint, cilantro, chickpea flour, and toasted spices. Season with ½ teaspoon salt and a few grinds of black pepper, and mix well. If you are using winter squash, stir in a pinch each of ground cinnamon and ground ginger. (The pancake batter can be made up to 2 days ahead and stored, covered, in the fridge.)

Heat a large skillet, preferably cast iron, over medium-high heat for a minute or two. Add the butter, then spoon in two overflowing ½ cupfuls (120 ml) of the pancake batter, pressing each to ½ inch (12 mm) thick. Cook, rotating the skillet occasionally for even browning, until the pancakes are nicely browned, about 3 minutes. Flip, then cook the second side for another few minutes. Transfer the pancakes to a plate. Repeat to make two more pancakes, adding more butter to the skillet, if needed.

Season the labneh with salt.

Just before serving, toss the greens with the lemon juice, oil, and some salt and pepper. Top each socca pancake with a huge dollop of labneh and a tangle of greens.

NOTE ON THE WINTER SQUASH

You can use any kind of winter squash that you like. We usually go for kabocha. If you're having a hard time grating the squash on one of those handheld box graters, try cutting the squash into 2-inch (5-cm) pieces and then shredding them in a food processor.

WANT TO MAKE IT HEARTIER?

Add a fried egg on top.

SPICE UP THE LABNEH

Have fun with the seasoning. Try mixing in ras el hanout or za'atar.

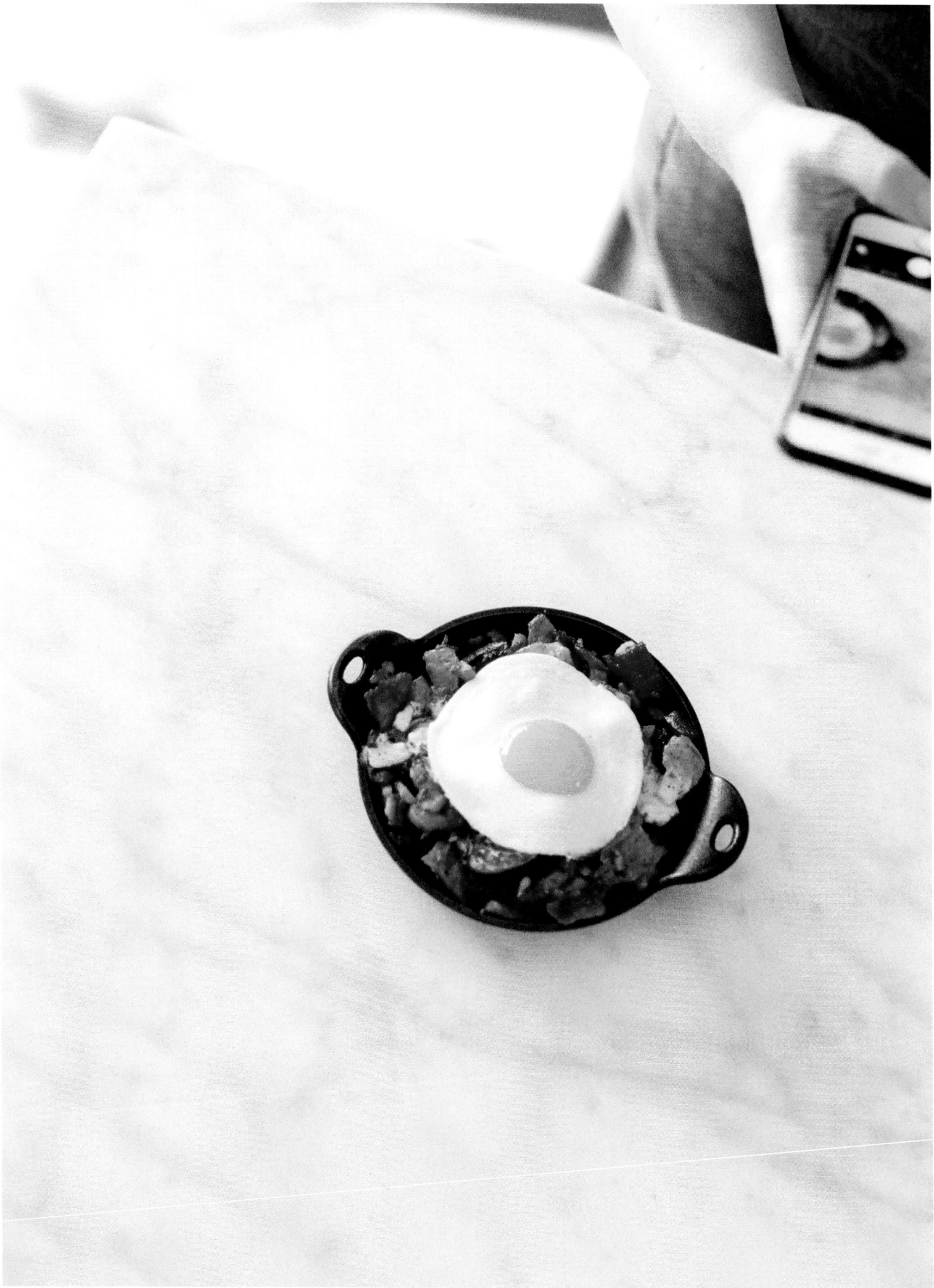

Seasonal hash

Seasonal hash
Red flannel hash with horseradish crème fraîche

Think of this hash as something to top with a fried egg and eat for breakfast, or as a side dish (without the egg) to enjoy with dinner. Just make sure the hash is GBD. Golden. Brown. Delicious.

Serves 2 very hungry people or 3 not-so-hungry people (V, GF)

2 Yukon Gold potatoes (about 8 ounces/225 g total), scrubbed

2 or 3 beets (about 8 ounces/225 g total), scrubbed

2 tablespoons extra-virgin olive oil, plus more as needed

Fine sea salt and freshly ground black pepper

1 large red onion, quartered

½ cup (120 ml) crème fraîche (page 265 or store-bought)

2 tablespoons grated horseradish

½ lemon

½ cup (100 g) shredded corned beef (optional)

3 scallions, thinly sliced on the bias

¾ cup (60 g) grated dry Jack or cheddar cheese

2 tablespoons unsalted butter, plus more as needed

2 fried eggs (page 22)

Preheat the oven to 425°F (220°C). Rub the potatoes and beets with a bit of oil, sprinkle with salt and pepper, and wrap individually in aluminum foil. Put on a rimmed baking sheet and roast until they can be easily pierced with a fork, 40 to 60 minutes, depending on their size. (If the potatoes and beets are different sizes, remove each as it is done.)

About halfway into the baking time, toss the onion quarters in enough oil to coat, then add to the baking sheet with the potatoes and beets and roast, turning occasionally, until tender and a little caramelized, 20 to 25 minutes.

In a small bowl, stir together the crème fraîche and horseradish. Season with salt, pepper, and lemon juice.

When the potatoes are cool enough to handle, crush and tear them by hand. Peel and trim the beets, then chop them to about the same size as the potato pieces. Do the same with the onions. Mix the vegetables with the corned beef, if you're using it, along with the scallions, cheese, and a pinch each of salt and pepper.

Set a large skillet over medium heat, then add 2 tablespoons oil and the butter. When the pan is hot but not smoking, add the potato-beet mixture and sprinkle with salt and pepper. Shake the skillet to form a single layer, then cook the hash undisturbed, adjusting the heat as necessary so that the vegetables sizzle and bubble. If the pan looks dry, add more butter, but not so much that the hash starts to look oily. Cook until the potatoes and beets are light golden brown on the bottom,

5 to 10 minutes. (There's so much moisture in the beets that they don't really have the ability to caramelize deeply.) Turn the hash over, then sprinkle the browned sides with salt and remove from the heat.

Serve the hash in the skillet, topped with a good squeeze of lemon juice, a friendly schmear of the horseradish crème fraîche, and the fried eggs.

ACCOMPANIMENT

Serve with a salad of small, leafy mixed lettuces tossed with lemon juice and Everyday Mustard Vinaigrette (page 265).

SHISHITO-TOMATILLO VARIATION

Omit the beets and use 4 potatoes (about 1 pound/455 g total). Instead of the red onion, use 1 leek, cleaned well and sliced ¼ inch (6 mm) thick.

Thinly slice 2 heaping cups (115 g) stemmed shishito peppers and add them when you mix in the cheese. Instead of horseradish crème fraîche, make a tomatillo sauce: Roast 1½ pounds (680 g) husked tomatillos, 8 ounces (225 g) tomatoes, 3 garlic cloves, and ½ yellow onion on a rimmed baking sheet in a 400°F (205°C) oven until collapsed and browned. Puree along with the leaves from ½ bunch fresh cilantro, then transfer to a pot and simmer for 10 minutes. Season with fresh lime juice and salt. To serve, drizzle tomatillo sauce over the hash.

SQUASH AND GREEN HARISSA VARIATION

Omit the beets and use 4 potatoes (about 1 pound/455 g total). Cut 1 to 2 delicata squash (about 1 pound/455 g total) in half lengthwise, then scoop out and discard the seeds. Slice the squash into half-moons ½ inch (12 mm) thick. Toss them with enough olive oil to coat and a few pinches of salt, and roast them on a baking sheet in the oven with the potatoes until lightly caramelized and tender, about 15 minutes. Instead of the red onion, use 1 leek, cleaned well and sliced ¼ inch (6 mm) thick. Swap out the horseradish crème fraîche for a green harissa. Here's how to make it: In a blender, puree 3 garlic cloves, 1 seeded and stemmed jalapeño, 1 tablespoon toasted and ground cumin, 1 teaspoon toasted and ground coriander, ½ cup (120 ml) fresh lemon juice, and 1½ teaspoons salt. Cut the bottom stems off 1 bunch fresh cilantro and 1 bunch fresh parsley, and add the leafy tops to the blender. Blend. While the blade is spinning, slowly drizzle in ½ cup (120 ml) olive oil.

Bipolar Shishitos

Tomato party

tomato (paste, powder, and stem oil) salad with whipped feta and garlic chips

At its core, this salad is made up of a few central components: tomato paste, whipped feta, fresh tomatoes, plus a drizzle of flavorful oil. If you're feeling really ambitious, you can use the tomato juices and pulp to make the paste, and the tomato stems and leaves to make the oil. You could also make a powder from the leftover tomato skins and seeds. On the other hand, if you'd rather cut to the chase, just buy the best tomato paste you can find and use super good olive oil for the final drizzle.

Serves 4 to 6 (V, GF)

FOR THE TOMATO STEM OIL, TOMATO POWDER, AND TOMATO PASTE (ALL OPTIONAL)

¾ cup (180 ml) non-GMO canola or other neutral-flavored oil
4 pounds (1.8 kg) sauce tomatoes (such as San Marzano or Early Girl), on the vine
Leaves from ½ bunch fresh parsley
Fine sea salt

FOR THE WHIPPED FETA

1 cup (115 g) sheep's-milk feta
Buttermilk, as needed
Fine sea salt and freshly ground black pepper

FOR THE GARLIC CHIPS (OPTIONAL)

6 to 8 cloves garlic
Clarified butter (for frying; about 3 cups/720 ml)
Fine sea salt

TO SERVE

2 pints (1 pound 4 ounces/565 g) cherry tomatoes, halved
1 tablespoon sherry vinegar
3 tablespoons fresh flat-leaf parsley leaves
1 tablespoon chopped fresh dill
¼ cup (15 g) fresh opal basil leaves
Fine sea salt and freshly ground black pepper

MAKE THE TOMATO STEM OIL

Pour the oil into a jar and place in the freezer to chill while you prepare the other ingredients. Pick all the stems and leaves from the tomatoes and coarsely chop them. You'll need ½ cup (50 g) chopped stems and leaves. Bring a pot of water to a rolling boil. Fill a bowl with ice water and keep it nearby. Blanch the stems and leaves for 30 seconds in the boiling water, then transfer to the ice bath. Blanch the parsley for 15 seconds, then transfer to the ice bath. Lift out and squeeze all the green things until there is no moisture left. Squeeze them again and again. Use a towel. Use your muscles. There can be no residual water.

Using a high-speed blender, blend the green things and the chilled oil together on high speed until the greens are completely pureed. Strain through a cheesecloth-lined sieve for at least 2 hours, or overnight.

MAKE THE TOMATO POWDER

Chop the tomatoes, then pass them through a food mill. Spread the seeds and skins out on a dehydrator tray. Set the dehydrator to 135°F (57°C) and leave the seeds and skins to dry out overnight or until they are crisp and no longer chewy. To finish the tomato powder, blitz the dehydrated skins and seeds in a high-speed blender on high speed.

MAKE THE TOMATO PASTE

Transfer all the milled tomato juice and pulp to a nonreactive pot and bring to a simmer. Cook until the tomatoes have the consistency of pizza sauce, about 30 minutes. Pour the sauce into a heat-safe container that is wide enough for the sauce to be 2 to 3 inches (5 to 7.5 cm) deep. Dehydrate at 135°F (57°C), stirring twice daily, until the sauce has turned into a thick paste, 3 to 5 days. To finish the tomato paste, blend the paste in a food processor or blender for several minutes, until completely smooth. Taste and season with as much salt as you like.

MAKE THE WHIPPED FETA

Crumble the feta into the bowl of a food processor fitted with a metal blade. Blend until the feta won't

move, 5 to 10 seconds. While the blade is spinning, slowly pour in buttermilk, stopping as soon as the feta begins moving freely again. Blend for 2 minutes, stopping once to scrape down the sides and bottom with a rubber spatula. The whipped feta should be thick and creamy with the smooth consistency of crème fraîche and the surprisingly tangy flavor of feta. Season with salt and pepper.

MAKE THE GARLIC CHIPS

Slice the garlic crosswise as thinly and evenly as you possibly can. (Carefully use a mandoline, if you have one.) Fill a small pot with at least 2 inches (5 cm) of clarified butter, then heat the butter to 300°F (150°C). Drop in the garlic slices and cook them for about 6 minutes. If they turn dark brown right away, the butter is too hot and the chips will taste bitter. You want them to brown slowly. When the garlic chips are all golden blond, transfer them to a paper towel–lined plate, sprinkle with salt, and

let cool. (You can filter and save the butter for another use.)

ASSEMBLE THE TOMATO SALAD

In a large bowl, toss the cherry tomatoes with the vinegar, parsley, dill, and basil. Season with salt and pepper. Schmear some tomato paste in an arc on a large platter or individual plates, then spread the whipped feta over the paste to hide it. Arrange the cherry tomato mixture on top of the feta. Drizzle on the stem oil (or super-good olive oil, if that's what you're using), scatter on the garlic chips, and sprinkle a big pinch of tomato powder over everything, including the edge of the plate, so you can see the color of the powder.

POSSIBLE ADDITIONS

If you like, sprinkle crunchy quinoa (page 165) over the salad for texture. Bloomsdale spinach leaves or Red Frill mustard (as shown in the photo on page 98) would also be great mixed in with the cherry tomatoes.

Shhh . . . Basil at The Garden Of . . . .

Stinging nettle cavatelli

Stinging nettle cavatelli
green flecked pasta, crispy spigarello, and garlic

Our cook Paul Everett is our pasta guy. The pasta he makes is always supple, never overworked. This cavatelli dish is one of the best dishes to have come from his magic pasta fingers.

Serves 6 to 8 (V)

2 bunches (about 1½ pounds/680 g) spigarello **(see Note)**
4 tablespoons (60 ml) extra-virgin olive oil, plus more as needed
Fine sea salt
5 cups (100 g) stinging nettles **(see Note)**
1½ cups (340 g) drained ricotta (page 268 or store-bought)
2 large eggs, beaten

3 cups (375 g) all-purpose flour
Semolina, as needed
4 cloves garlic, sliced
½ teaspoon dried chile pepper flakes (optional)
½ cup (120 ml) white wine
¼ cup (60 ml) heavy cream
Cracked black pepper
Finely grated Parmigiano cheese, for serving (optional)

Preheat the oven to 350°F (175°C).

Trim the spigarello, removing the tough bottom part of the stems, then cut into big bite-size pieces. Rub with enough oil to coat, sprinkle with a few pinches of salt, and spread out on a rimmed baking sheet. Roast until crisp and golden brown around the edges but still green in the center of the thickest stem.

Meanwhile, make the cavatelli: Fill a medium bowl with ice water. Bring a large pot of salted water to a boil. Using tongs, pick up the nettles and drop them into the pot. Cook for 1 minute, then immediately transfer to the ice bath. (You can keep the pot of hot water going to boil the pasta later on.) Let the greens cool, then gently squeeze out all the water—it's safe to use your bare hands now. Using a food processor or a blender, puree the nettles along with 2 tablespoons of the oil and a pinch of salt. (Alternatively, you could use a knife to chop them very, very finely, although this will take some time.) Add the ricotta and beaten eggs to the nettle puree and blend until the mixture is light and fluffy.

Measure the flour into a large bowl, make a deep well in the center, and pour the nettle mixture into the well. Using a fork, slowly stir the well and gradually pull flour into the well, a little at a time, until most of the flour has been mixed in and your hand feels like it is going to fall off. Dump the shaggy mixture out onto a cutting board and knead it just until all the flour has been incorporated and the dough is smooth and bouncy. Cover and let it rest at room temperature for 30 minutes.

Scatter a little semolina, if you have it (or flour, if you don't), across two parchment paper–lined baking sheets. Divide the dough into 8 equal pieces. Using both hands, roll each piece into a long snake about the thickness of your pointer finger. Cut it crosswise into 1-inch (2.5-cm) segments. Pick up one segment at a time and press it with your thumb against a wooden gnocchi board or against the back of a fork, rolling it off to create ridges on one side and a little crater on the side where your thumb was. Flick each ridged segment onto the prepared baking sheets. Don't stack or pile the cavatelli because they will definitely stick.

Bring the pot of water to a gentle boil. Add a few big pinches of salt.

While the water heats up, set a large pan over medium heat. Swirl in the remaining 2 tablespoons oil, then add the garlic, pepper flakes, and ¾ teaspoon salt. Cook, stirring often, until the garlic is soft but not yet brown, about 1 minute. Pour in the wine, let it bubble ferociously for 30 seconds, then pour in the cream. Cook the sauce until it has reduced a bit and coats the back of a wooden spoon, about 5 minutes.

Once the water in the pot is bubbling, drop in the cavatelli. As soon as they float to the surface, skim them up using a slotted spoon and transfer to the sauce. Ladle some of the pasta-cooking water into the sauce. Toss well to coat the pasta and season with salt.

Serve in warm shallow bowls, with the crispy spigarello piled on top. Shower each bowl generously with black pepper and cheese, if desired.

DON'T FEEL LIKE ROASTING SPIGARELLO?

Just quickly sauté a couple of big handfuls of stemmed kale leaves and serve those on top of the pasta instead.

NOTE ON STINGING NETTLES

Please don't use your hands to measure the nettles—these nettles sting! Weigh them, if you want to be precise, or just eyeball it.

CAN'T FIND STINGING NETTLES?

Use spinach!

IS MAKING CAVATELLI NOT ON THE AGENDA FOR TONIGHT?

I get it. There are a lot of steps involved. Go to the store and buy a couple of packages of gnocchi, make the spigarello, then skip ahead to the pasta-boiling part.

Stinging nettle cavatelli

Chalchiuhtlicue, the Aztec Goddess of Water, aka Barbara Spencer

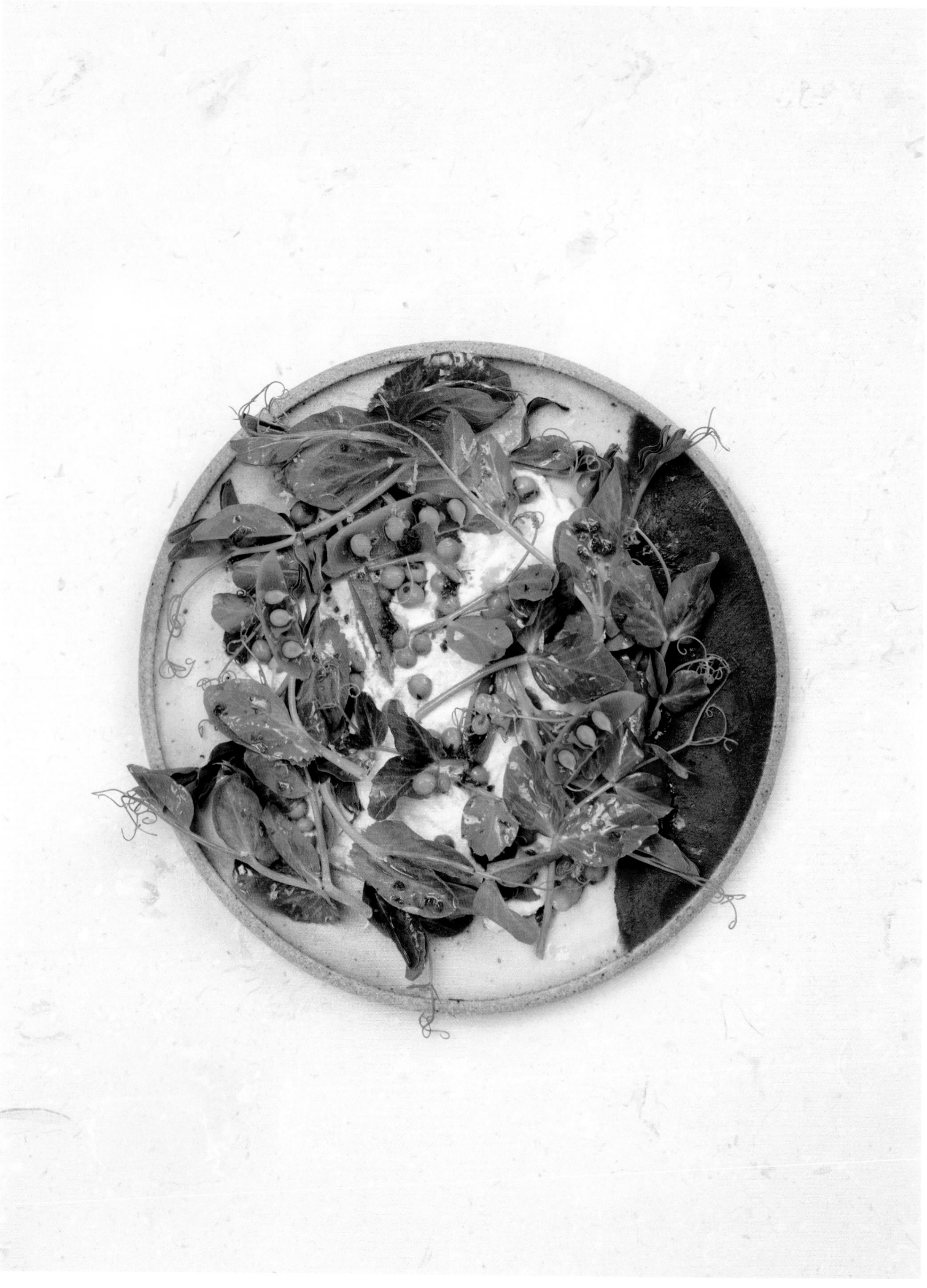

Super green spring

pea (English, snap, and tendrils) salad with date jam, Meyer lemon ricotta, and mint salsa verde

This is spring on a plate.

Serves 6 (GF, V, VVO)

FOR THE DATE JAM

1 cup (130 g) pitted dates
2 tablespoons apple cider vinegar
Fine sea salt

FOR THE MEYER LEMON RICOTTA

1 cup (240 ml) ricotta (page 268 or store-bought)
Zest and juice of ½ Meyer lemon
Pinch of fine sea salt

FOR THE MINT SALSA VERDE

½ small shallot, minced
1 tablespoon fresh lemon juice
1 tablespoon white wine vinegar
Fine sea salt
½ cup (25 g) finely chopped fresh mint
¼ cup (13 g) finely chopped fresh flat-leaf
   parsley
4 salt-packed capers, rinsed and chopped
½ cup (120 ml) extra-virgin olive oil

FOR THE PEAS

3¾ cups (225 g) snap peas
1 cup (170 g) shelled fresh English peas (from
   1 pound/455 g in the pod)
2 small bunches (280 g) pea tendrils

TO SERVE

½ Meyer lemon
Really good olive oil
Fleur de sel

MAKE THE DATE JAM

Place the dates in a small pot and cover with at least 1 inch (2.5 cm) of water. Simmer until falling-apart tender, about 6 minutes. Drain in a fine-mesh sieve, then transfer to a small bowl. Use a fork to mash the dates to a rough puree. If you have a mortar and pestle, that is an even better way to pound the dates smooth. (At the restaurant, we make big batches and blend the dates in a food processor until super smooth and pipe-able.) If you like, you can triple or quadruple this recipe to make a big batch. Date jam is wonderful stirred into plain yogurt or schmeared on toast and sprinkled with ground cinnamon.

Mix in the apple cider vinegar and season with salt to taste. (If making ahead, store, covered, in the refrigerator for up to 2 weeks.)

MAKE THE MEYER LEMON RICOTTA

In a bowl, stir together the ricotta, lemon zest, a squeeze of the lemon juice, and salt. Taste, adding a bit more lemon juice and/or salt, if desired. (If making ahead, store, covered, in the refrigerator for up to 2 days.)

MAKE THE MINT SALSA VERDE

Combine the shallot, lemon juice, white wine vinegar, and a tiny pinch of salt in a medium bowl. Let the shallot soften for about 5 minutes. Stir in the mint, parsley, capers, and oil. Taste and adjust the seasonings as you like. (If making ahead, pour a ½-inch/12-mm-deep cap of olive oil over the salsa verde and store, covered, in the refrigerator for up to 3 days.)

MAKE THE PEAS

Bring a pot of salted water to a boil. Fill a bowl with ice water and keep it nearby. Snip off the ends of the snap peas and remove their strings. Slice them thinly on the bias. Boil the snap peas and English peas for 10 seconds, then use a slotted spoon to drop them into the ice water and let cool completely. Drain, then spread out on paper towels to dry.

To serve, in a large bowl, toss the snap peas, English peas, and pea tendrils with a big squeeze of Meyer lemon juice, a drizzle of oil, and a generous pinch of fleur de sel. Smear some of the date jam across the bottom of six plates or a large platter. Spread the Meyer lemon ricotta on top of the date jam. Divide the pea salad among the plates, using your fingers to lift the salad and give it some good height. Drizzle some mint salsa verde over each salad.

GOT A SMOKER?
At Sqirl we like to smoke the dates before turning them into jam.

Super green spring

Shu Takikawa of The Garden Of . . .

"We pick our corn and lettuces at the crack
of dawn to ensure the corn's sweetness and
lettuces that stay fresh to their core. This is
what people don't know . . . what happens from
the time it is harvested to the time it gets to the
person you're selling it to . . . that time determines
a huge amount of the value and quality of
the product. And it's not about the time frame
(in which it is picked), but the temperature."

Saturday, April 10th at 5 pm. Debby Takikawa in conversation with Jessica Koslow

Meat
112—149

Most dishes we serve at Sqirl are vegetarian or vegetable-focused, so I try to make the few meat dishes that we do offer feel really special. For me, this starts with buying from producers who respect the animals and the land, and ends with savoring meat as the true luxury that it is. If you've ever wanted to make your own bacon at home, now is your chance. The reward? You'll know it when you smell this bacon cooking at home. In this chapter I've included a wide range of meat dishes from classics like breakfast sausage to unexpected curiosities like rabbit ballotine.

Cured (not smoked) bacon

Cured (not smoked) bacon

Like just about everyone, I love and enjoy a good smoked bacon. There's one small problem with making it at the restaurant: We don't have the facilities to smoke the huge quantity of bacon we serve. So what we do instead is cure pork belly with salt and a mix of spices, then cook it slowly in a low oven. Fortunately, this recipe is relatively easy to re-create at home.

Makes about 35 (¼-inch/6-mm) slices (GF)

⅓ cup (70 g) fine sea salt
¼ cup (65 g) packed brown sugar
Leaves from 12 sprigs fresh thyme
5 cloves garlic, minced
3 tablespoons molasses
2 teaspoons freshly ground black pepper
5 pounds (2.3 kg) pork belly, skin removed

In a bowl, combine the salt, sugar, thyme, garlic, molasses, and pepper. Mix well. Massage half this mixture onto one side of the belly. Flip, and massage the other half onto the other side. Put the belly on a rimmed baking sheet, cover with plastic wrap, and place in the refrigerator to cure for 7 days. Flip the belly once every other day. You could set an alarm to ensure flip-timing consistency. However, if you miss a day, all will not be lost.

Rinse off the salt cure and pat the belly dry. Preheat the oven to 200°F (90°C).

Place the cured bacon on a wire rack set inside a rimmed baking sheet. Bake until the internal temperature of the bacon reaches 145°F (63°C), 2 to 3 hours.

Once the bacon is done, turn up the oven temperature to 500°F (260°C) and let the bacon get nicely browned, about 10 minutes. Remove from the oven and let cool completely.

Cut the bacon into slices ¼ inch (6 mm) thick. (We like our bacon thick.) Cook in a medium-hot pan until crisp. We use a cast-iron steak weight to press down on the bacon while it cooks and keep it flat. You could use a brick wrapped in aluminum foil or even a small ramekin.

Store any uncooked bacon, covered, in the refrigerator for up to 2 weeks or in the freezer, well wrapped, for up to 3 months.

Breakfast sausage

This breakfast sausage isn't exactly what you'd imagine it to be; it's not Jimmy Dean. It's more like a dinnertime fennel sausage. I wanted to come up with something that wasn't too sweet, something savory that would go with everything else on our menu.

Makes 12 to 14 (2-inch/5-cm) patties (GF)

2 pounds (910 g) pork shoulder (or pre-ground)
1 tablespoon fennel seeds
½ teaspoon freshly ground black pepper
2 teaspoons fine sea salt
1 tablespoon rice vinegar
1½ teaspoons dried chile pepper flakes
Pinch of paprika
2 cloves garlic, peeled
Olive oil, as needed

TO GRIND THE MEAT

Cut the pork into 1-inch (2.5-cm) cubes, trimming and discarding any fibrous sinew. Spread the cubes out on a parchment paper–lined rimmed baking sheet. Freeze until the edges of the cubes are rigid but the middles are still pliable, about 30 minutes.

Meanwhile, toast the fennel seeds in a small, dry pan set over medium heat for a few minutes, or just until they begin turning golden brown.

In a large bowl, combine the black pepper, salt, vinegar, and ¼ cup (60 ml) water.

Once the meat is sufficiently cold, sprinkle the toasted fennel seeds, chile flakes, and paprika over the meat, then push the seasoned meat and the garlic cloves through a meat grinder fitted with a medium-fine die (³⁄₁₆-inch/5-mm hole size). Alternatively, use a food processor fitted with a metal blade to grind the seasoned meat and garlic, filling the bowl of the processor only halfway and working in batches to pulse the meat to a fine grind. Add the ground pork to the bowl with the spice slurry.

IF YOU ARE USING PRE-GROUND MEAT

Put it in a large bowl with all the seasonings. (You will need to first toast the fennel seeds as instructed and grind them using a mortar and pestle or a spice grinder. You will also need to mince the garlic before adding to the bowl.) Use your hands to mix everything together for a minute or two, until the meat has a tacky texture and the spices are well incorporated. (The meat will be freezing cold, so use a spoon, if you prefer.)

Shape the meat mixture into 2½-ounce (70-g) patties about 1 inch (2.5 cm) thick and a little more than 2 inches (5 cm) across.

Heat a wide skillet over medium-high heat for 1 minute. Add enough oil to coat the bottom of the skillet, then add as many sausage patties as will fit without crowding. Sear until nicely caramelized on the first side, 3 to 4 minutes. Flip, and sear the second side just until the sausages are cooked through, another 3 to 4 minutes. Transfer the cooked sausages to a plate. Continue cooking the patties, adding oil to the pan as needed to prevent burning. The second batch will cook a bit faster than the first.

Store any uncooked patties, covered, in the refrigerator for up to 3 days or in the freezer, tightly wrapped, for up to 3 months.

Chicken kofte on rosemary sprigs with garlic schmear and cabbage kumquat salad

Chicken kofte on rosemary sprigs with garlic schmear and cabbage kumquat salad

If you've lived in Los Angeles anytime in the past thirty years, you've probably been to Zankou Chicken and eaten their revelatory garlicky white sauce. While they do serve shawarma and kabobs, I never stray from my usual order of the meal combo of roast chicken with a side of cabbage salad, and extra white sauce. True love is when two people can eat that sauce within three feet of each other. Inspired by those flavors, I came up with this dish, an homage to Zankou, Sqirl-ified.

Serves 6 (GF)

FOR THE GARLIC SCHMEAR

30 cloves garlic
1½ teaspoons fine sea salt
3 tablespoons fresh lemon juice
1¼ cups (300 ml) non-GMO canola oil

FOR THE CABBAGE KUMQUAT SALAD

10 kumquats
3 tablespoons fresh lemon juice
¼ cup (60 ml) extra-virgin olive oil
1 teaspoon dried oregano
Fine sea salt
½ green cabbage (14 ounces/400 g)
¼ cup (13 g) loosely packed fresh mint leaves,
  thinly sliced

FOR THE CHICKEN KOFTE

1 pound 10 ounces (750 g) ground chicken
¼ cup (60 ml) red wine
2 small roasted red peppers, finely chopped
3 sprigs fresh thyme, stemmed
3 cloves garlic, minced
¾ teaspoon mild chile powder
½ teaspoon smoked paprika
¼ teaspoon freshly ground black pepper
2 teaspoons fine sea salt
12 thick fresh rosemary sprigs, leaves stripped
  from bottom two-thirds of each
2 tablespoons olive oil, plus more as needed

MAKE THE GARLIC SCHMEAR

In the bowl of a food processor fitted with a metal blade, combine the garlic, salt, lemon juice, and 3 tablespoons water. Puree until very finely chopped, stopping to scrape down the sides of the bowl as needed. With the motor running, gradually pour in the oil, drop by drop at first, then in a very thin stream. How slowly can you go? Let the blade spin for a little while and take your time, up to 10 minutes of it. Emulsification plus patience create this magic fluffy schmear. There will be more garlic schmear than you'll need for six servings. (We tried making a smaller batch but it didn't emulsify properly.) Fortunately, leftover schmear can be stored in an airtight container in the refrigerator for several weeks.

MAKE THE CABBAGE KUMQUAT SALAD

Cut the kumquats in half at their waists. Roll each half away from you, pressing gently to squeeze out the seeds. In the bowl of a blender or a food processor, combine the kumquat pieces, lemon juice, oil, oregano, and ¼ teaspoon salt. Puree until smooth.

Cut out the core of the cabbage. Slice the cabbage as thinly as possible. (We use a mandoline, but a sharp knife will do.) In a large bowl, toss the cabbage with the mint and most of the kumquat dressing. Taste and add more salt or dressing, as needed.

MAKE THE CHICKEN KOFTE

Preheat the oven to 400°F (205°C).

In a bowl, combine the chicken, wine, roasted peppers, thyme, garlic, chile powder, paprika, black pepper, and salt. Mix well. Mold the mixture evenly around the rosemary sprigs to form cylinders, using about 2½ ounces (70 grams) for each.

Heat the oil in a large skillet over medium-high heat. Lay as many chicken skewers as will fit in a single layer in the pan and sear them until browned on all sides, about 4 minutes total. Transfer to a rimmed baking sheet. Repeat the searing process, adding oil as needed, until you've browned all the kofte. Roast in the oven until the center of each one is just cooked through, about 5 minutes.

To serve, spread some garlic schmear on six plates. Divide the cabbage kumquat salad among the plates, piling it atop the schmear, then lay two kofte skewers next to each salad.

WHAT'S THIS PLATE MISSING?
A bowl of buttered rice.

Chicken kofte on rosemary sprigs with garlic schmear and cabbage kumquat salad

Hey, I'm walking here. Schaner Family Farms.

Roasted chicken salad with market greens, garbanzos, and soft-boiled eggs

Roasted chicken salad with market greens, garbanzos, and soft-boiled eggs

I was first introduced to cream dressing when I lived in Atlanta. You hear the word *cream* next to the word *dressing* and you imagine heavy things. But people use olive oil in salad dressing, and that's not so different. Cream has its own clean and bright flavor, and you don't need to add that much to give the dressing a smooth, rounded texture. I guess what I'm trying to say is, don't be afraid of the cream.

Serves 6 (GFO)

2 large bone-in chicken breasts
 (1½ pounds/680 g total), skin on
1 tablespoon olive oil
Fine sea salt and freshly ground black pepper
2 large watermelon radishes (8 ounces/225 g
 total)
1½ cups (240 g) cooked garbanzos (page 69)
6 cups (300 g) small, leafy mixed lettuces,
 cleaned and torn
½ cup (120 ml) Southern-Style Fresh Cream
 and Black Mustard Dressing (page 266)
1 lemon, halved
3 soft-boiled eggs (page 22), halved
6 slices *rugbrød* or other dense health bread,
 toasted

Preheat the oven to 425°F (220°C).

Put the chicken on a rimmed baking sheet, rub with the oil, and season with ½ teaspoon salt and a few grinds of pepper. Roast until cooked through, 30 to 35 minutes. Let cool, then shred the meat into bite-size pieces, discarding the skin and bones.

Cut the radishes into cubes about the same size as the garbanzos and toss them into a large bowl. Add the chicken, garbanzos, greens, about three-quarters of the dressing, a big squeeze of lemon juice, and ¼ teaspoon salt. Toss well, then taste. Add a bit more salt, dressing, and lemon juice, if desired. The greens should be well coated and there

should be enough lemon juice that you can taste a little zing.

Serve with the eggs and *rugbrød*. Feel free to soft-boil 6 eggs and serve 2 halves per plate, if you want.

WANT TO MAKE THIS GLUTEN FREE?
Don't eat the bread.

Beef ravioli with carrot sauce and celery leaf pesto

Beef ravioli with carrot sauce and celery leaf pesto

This ravioli dough is pretty luxurious. It's based on pierogi dough, with cream cheese for added silkiness. You can use any kind of cooked beef to fill the ravioli. Maybe leftovers from Ramos-Style Short Ribs and Vegetables in Beef Consommé (page 147) or some shredded brisket?

Makes about 24 ravioli; serves 4 to 6

FOR THE BEEF RAVIOLI

3 tablespoons cream cheese
1 large egg
3 cups (375 g) all-purpose flour, plus more for rolling
1 teaspoon fine sea salt
1¾ cups (175 g) shredded cooked beef, chopped

FOR THE CARROT SAUCE

¼ cup (60 ml) beef fat or olive oil
1 yellow onion, thinly sliced
1 stalk celery, diced
3 cloves garlic, smashed
3 fresh sage leaves, torn
½ cup (120 ml) white wine
4 large carrots (14 ounces/400 g total), peeled and cut into 1-inch (2.5-cm) pieces, plus 1 large carrot (100 g), peeled
Fine sea salt
3 tablespoons unsalted butter

FOR THE CELERY LEAF PESTO

1 cup (20 g) loosely packed celery leaves (mostly from the center of the head)
½ cup (10 g) loosely packed fresh parsley leaves
¼ cup (60 ml) extra-virgin olive oil
Grated zest of 1 lemon
¼ cup (30 g) chopped toasted almonds
Fine sea salt

TO SERVE

Fine sea salt
2 tablespoons unsalted butter
Grated Parmigiano-Reggiano or pecorino cheese
Tiny fresh opal basil leaves or torn bigger basil leaves (optional)
½ lemon
Freshly ground black pepper
Fleur de sel
Fennel fronds (optional)

MAKE THE BEEF RAVIOLI

Combine the cream cheese and egg in a large bowl and use a wooden spoon to mix well. Add the flour, salt, and ⅔ cup (165 ml) water and stir until a shaggy dough forms. Turn it out onto an unfloured work surface and knead with your hands for 1 minute, just until smooth, being careful not to overwork the dough. Wrap in plastic and refrigerate for 1 hour.

On a floured surface, roll out the dough to ⅛ inch (4 mm) thick using a rolling pin. Cut the dough into long sheets 3 inches (7.5 cm) wide. Place 1-tablespoon dollops of shredded beef along the center of each dough sheet, spacing the dollops 1 inch (2.5 cm) apart. Lightly brush the exposed dough with water, then fold each sheet lengthwise and press firmly to seal. Run your fingers around each mound of filling to squeeze out any trapped air. Using a pasta-cutting wheel or knife, cut each sheet into individual ravioli. If you used a knife, crimp the edges of each raviolo with a fork. (Ravioli can be made ahead and stored in a single layer—no touching, or they'll stick!—on a baking sheet lined with parchment paper for up to 2 days in the fridge.)

Beef ravioli with carrot sauce and celery leaf pesto

MAKE THE CARROT SAUCE

Set a pot over medium heat. Add the fat, onion, and celery, and cook, stirring often, until softened, about 3 minutes. Add the garlic and sage and cook for another 2 minutes. Pour in the wine and let it boil until it reduces in volume by about half, then add the chopped carrots plus enough water to just barely cover. Season with salt—the liquid should taste a little saltier than soup. Simmer until the carrots are tender all the way through, about 25 minutes. Puree the mixture in a blender until very smooth.

Chop the remaining carrot into tiny (about ⅛ inch/3 mm) dice. Heat a pan over medium-low heat. Add the butter, then add the carrot dice and season with a pinch of salt. Cook gently, stirring, until tender. Remove from the heat and set aside.

MAKE THE CELERY LEAF PESTO

Chop the celery leaves and parsley very finely and place them in a bowl. Stir in the oil, lemon zest, almonds, and ¼ teaspoon salt. Taste, adding a bit more salt if needed.

When you're ready to serve, bring a pot of aggressively salted water to a boil. Heat the carrot sauce in a large pan over medium heat. Stir in the carrot dice and any butter left in the pan. Once the water boils, drop in the ravioli and cook until the pasta is tender, about 5 minutes. Using a slotted spoon, transfer the ravioli to the carrot sauce. Add a ladleful of pasta-cooking water to the sauce along with the butter and stir everything together until the butter has melted and the sauce has evenly coated the ravioli. Divide among warm plates. Top each with some grated cheese, a spoonful of celery leaf pesto, the basil (if you're using it), a generous squeeze of lemon juice, a few grinds of pepper, and a sprinkle of fleur de sel. Garnish with the fennel fronds.

"Our family has been taking care of this land for almost two hundred years. Every single year we have to listen to the environment and change as we go. We have to cut back or we have to grow based on the various elements at work . . . the water, the weather, the land . . . That has played a big part in defining our core values, what nature can provide each year. Then we set our own ranching and harvesting standards for our beef, with full transparency, leaving the consumer to decide if that's what they're wanting to buy."

Thursday, March 21st at 1 pm. Elizabeth Poett in conversation with Jessica Koslow

Elizabeth Poett's heyday

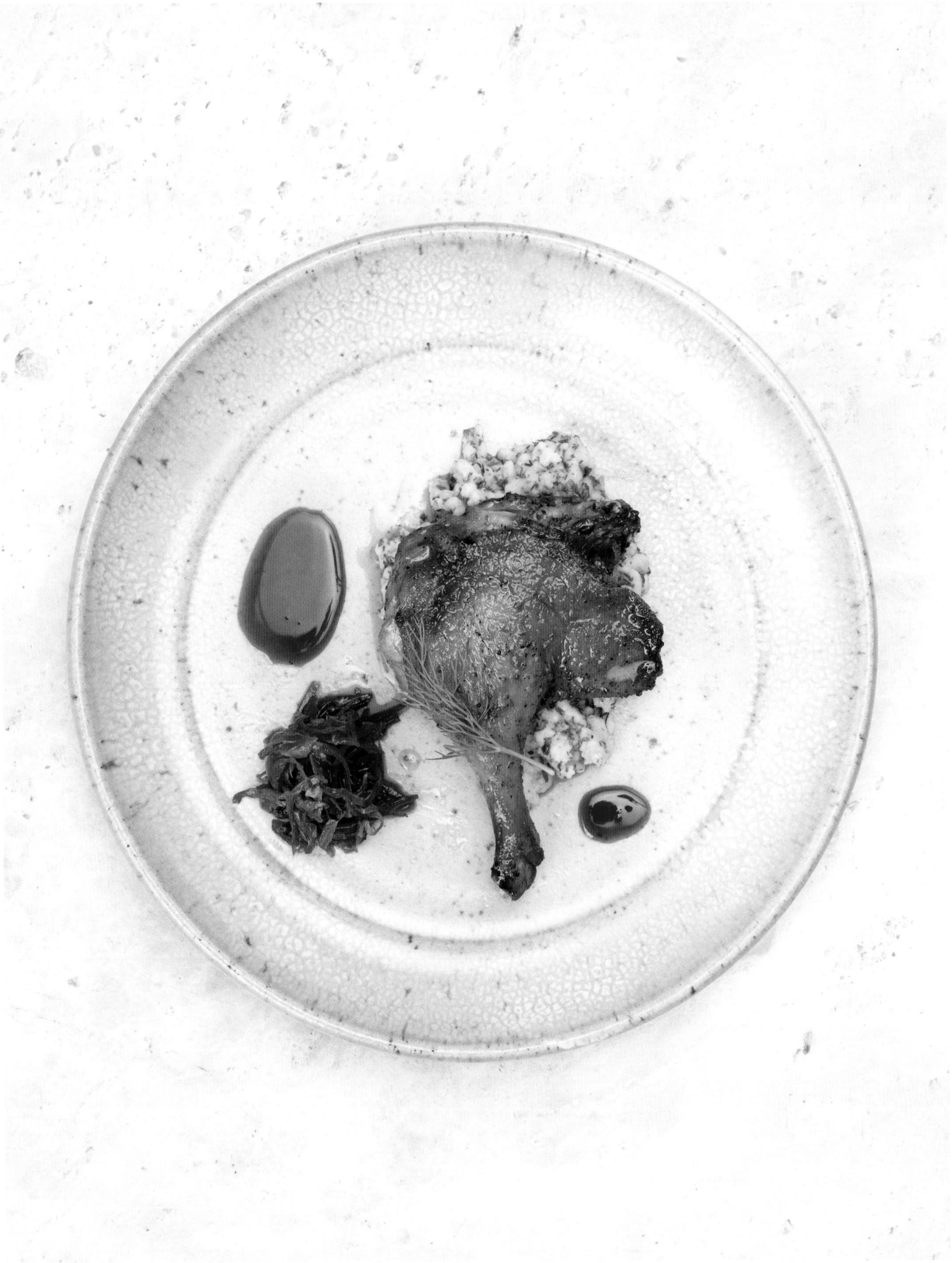

Braised duck legs with dill spätzle and sauerkraut

Braised duck legs with dill spätzle and sauerkraut

If you're really feeling the duck theme here, you could add a fried duck egg on top.
After making and eating all that, you might feel like you could chop down a tree.
(You could make any component of this dish by itself and it'd be quite delicious.)

Serves 6

FOR THE DUCK LEGS

6 duck legs (about 4 pounds/1.8 kg total),
   rinsed and patted dry
Fine sea salt and freshly ground black pepper
2 tablespoons extra-virgin olive oil
½ cup (120 ml) white verjus or crisp white wine
   (such as Muscadet)
4 cups (960 ml) duck stock (see Note) or good
   chicken stock, plus more as needed

FOR THE BRAISED SAUERKRAUT

3 tablespoons unsalted butter
½ medium yellow onion, finely chopped
2 stalks celery, finely chopped
½ teaspoon ground caraway
Fine sea salt
2 sprigs fresh thyme
1 bay leaf

⅓ cup (80 ml) white verjus or crisp white wine
   (such as Muscadet)
3 cups (400 g) drained sauerkraut made of red
   or green cabbage, rinsed well
2 tablespoons whole-grain mustard
Chicken or duck stock (see Note), as needed
   (about 2½ cups/600 ml)

FOR THE DILL SPÄTZLE

Fine sea salt
Olive oil
2 cups (250 g) all-purpose flour
1 cup (50 g) finely grated Parmigiano-Reggiano,
   Gruyère, or sharp cheddar cheese
¾ cup (38 g) finely chopped fresh dill
2 large eggs
¾ cup (180 ml) buttermilk, plus more as needed
2 cups (480 g) crème fraîche (page 265 or store-bought)
4 tablespoons (½ stick/55 g) unsalted butter

MAKE THE DUCK LEGS

Preheat the oven to 325°F (165°C).

Generously season the duck legs with salt and pepper on all sides. Set a Dutch oven over medium-high heat. Add the oil, then add as many duck legs, skin-side down, as will fit in a single layer without crowding. Cook for about 10 minutes, turning as needed if the skin extends over to the other side, until the skin is deep golden brown and crisp all over.

Transfer the legs to a plate, skin-side up, and repeat the browning process with the remaining legs. Be careful and don't put your face too close to the pot because duck has a lot of fat and it will sputter.

Once you've browned all the duck, pour off all but 1 tablespoon of the fat in the pot. (It's good! Keep it in an airtight container in the refrigerator for up to 6 months, and cook with it.) Pour the wine into the pot. Bring to a simmer, scraping the

bottom of the pot with a wooden spoon to release all the stuck browned bits. These add great flavor. Once the wine has reduced in volume by about half, add the stock and bring to a gentle simmer. Return the legs to the pot, skin-side up, and check to make sure that the liquid comes at least three-quarters of the way up the legs. If not, pour in a little more broth. Cover the pot and transfer to the oven. Braise until very tender, about 2 hours.

MAKE THE BRAISED SAUERKRAUT

Melt the butter in a heavy-bottomed pot over medium heat. Once the foaming subsides, add the onion, celery, caraway, and ¼ teaspoon salt. Tie the thyme and bay leaf together using kitchen twine and add to the pot. Cook, stirring often, until the vegetables have softened but aren't yet brown, about 4 minutes. Pour in the wine and let it cook for a minute or so. Stir in the sauerkraut and mustard, then add enough stock to almost but not quite cover the sauerkraut. Reduce the heat to low, cover the pot, and let simmer gently until the sauerkraut is tender, about 25 minutes. Discard the herb bundle. (Braised sauerkraut can be made ahead and stored in the fridge for up to 3 days.)

MAKE THE DILL SPÄTZLE

Bring a large pot of salted water to a boil. Lightly oil a rimmed baking sheet.

In a large bowl, whisk together the flour, cheese, ½ cup (25 g) of the dill, and 1 teaspoon salt. Make a well in the center of the flour mixture. In another bowl, beat the eggs, buttermilk, and crème fraîche, then pour the mixture into the well. Stir with a wooden spoon to combine. The spätzle batter will be loose but sticky—not like firm fresh pasta dough. If it's not quite as loose as cake batter, stir in additional buttermilk as needed.

Once the water is boiling rapidly, hold a colander over the pot, wearing oven mitts so you don't burn yourself, and scrape the batter directly into the colander. Use the wooden spoon to push the batter through the holes of the colander, letting little pieces of batter drop into the boiling water. Cook until the spätzle rise to the surface, less than 1 minute, then use a slotted spoon to transfer to the oil-slicked baking sheet. Don't stack them up too much because they'll stick. Let the cooked spätzle cool and firm up for a few minutes.

Preheat the oven to 375°F (190°C). Heat a wide cast-iron skillet over medium-high heat for 1 minute. Add 2 tablespoons of the butter and let it brown, then add about half the spätzle in a single layer. Resist the urge to nudge them around the pan; let them sear on one side for about 2 minutes. Using a spatula, turn them over and let them sear undisturbed on the second side for 2 minutes, until golden brown in a couple of places. Transfer to a platter. Add the remaining 2 tablespoons butter to the pan, followed by the other half of the spätzle. Cook in the same manner as the first batch. Sprinkle the remaining ¼ cup (13 g) dill over the top of the seared spätzle. Taste for seasoning, adding another pinch of salt, if needed.

Just before serving, place the duck legs on a baking sheet and into the preheated oven until the meat is heated through and the skin is crisp. Boil the duck braising liquid until slightly reduced in volume.

To serve, spoon hot spätzle onto six plates. Set one duck leg on top of each pile of spätzle. Arrange the braised sauerkraut alongside, and spoon a little of the duck braising juices onto each plate.

NOTE ON DUCK STOCK

You can use duck leg bones to make duck stock. To do so, roast a few pounds of duck bones on a rimmed baking sheet in a 425°F (220°C) oven until they're dark brown. Move them to a pot, cover with water, and bring to a boil. Skim any foam that rises to the surface. Simmer for 1 hour, then add a few garlic cloves, a few black peppercorns, 2 bay leaves, 4 sprigs thyme, and 1 cup (120 g) each of finely diced celery, carrot, and onion. Simmer until the stock is a deep chestnut color and tastes flavorful, about 1 hour more. Strain. Store in an airtight container in the refrigerator for up to 3 days or in the freezer for up to 3 months.

Braised duck legs with dill spätzle and sauerkraut

Family Meal, Windrose Farm

Lamb merguez with cranberry beans and slow-roasted tomatoes

Lamb merguez with cranberry beans and slow-roasted tomatoes

Lamb is lean, so you'll want to add a good amount of fat to it.
A good butcher will sell you some pork fatback, but if you can't get ahold of any,
no worries, try buying the thickest bacon you can find and using only the fat.

Serves 6 (GF)

FOR THE SLOW-ROASTED TOMATOES

6 small or 3 medium tomatoes (1 pound/
455 g total)
¼ cup (60 ml) extra-virgin olive oil
1 clove garlic, smashed
3 sprigs fresh resinous herbs (such as thyme,
rosemary, or sage)
Fine sea salt

FOR THE CRANBERRY BEANS

3 tablespoons extra-virgin olive oil
1-inch (2.5-cm) piece of ginger, peeled and
sliced
3 cloves garlic, smashed
1 bay leaf
1½ cups (280 g) dried cranberry beans
Fine sea salt

FOR THE LAMB MERGUEZ

1 pound 5 ounces (600 g) lamb shoulder or leg meat,
cut into 1-inch (2.5-cm) cubes (or pre-ground)
3 ounces (85 g) pork fatback, cut into 1-inch
cubes (or finely chopped)
1 teaspoon coriander seeds
1 teaspoon fennel seeds
¾ teaspoon cumin seeds
¾ teaspoon ground medium-hot chile pepper,
such as Aleppo, New Mexico, or guajillo
¾ teaspoon sweet paprika
Pinch of cayenne
Pinch of dried oregano
2 cloves garlic, peeled
Freshly ground black pepper
1 tablespoon red wine vinegar or sherry vinegar
1½ teaspoons fine sea salt
Extra-virgin olive oil

TO SERVE

½ cup (120 g) labneh (page 71 or store-bought)
¼ cup (13 g) loosely packed fresh mint leaves,
thinly sliced

MAKE THE SLOW-ROASTED TOMATOES

Preheat the oven to 300°F (150°C).

Remove any stems from the tomatoes and cut out any tough cores.

If the tomatoes are small, cut them in half through their equators. If they are medium, cut them in half through their equators and then cut each half into two or three wedges. Lay them skin-side down on a rimmed baking sheet. In a small pot

over low heat, warm the oil, garlic, and herb sprigs for a moment, just until the oil is infused with the garlic and herb flavors. Brush the cut sides of the tomatoes with the infused oil, reserving the remaining oil. Lightly season each wedge with a pinch of salt. Roast until concentrated, collapsed, and slightly browned, 1 to 2 hours. (Roasted tomatoes can be made ahead and stored in the infused oil, covered, in the refrigerator for up to 3 days. Otherwise, you don't need me to tell you that the leftover infused oil is delicious on many other things— such as grilled bread.)

MAKE THE CRANBERRY BEANS

Heat a large pot over medium heat. Swirl in the oil, then add the ginger, garlic, and bay leaf. Cook until the garlic and ginger are sizzling merrily and starting to barely brown, a minute or so. Add the beans to the pot, stirring to coat them in oil. Pour in enough water to cover the beans by a few inches and add 1 teaspoon salt. Adjust the heat so that the water barely simmers. Cook the beans until they are tender but not falling apart, 1 to 1½ hours, depending on how fresh the dried beans were. You may need to add a bit more water to keep the beans covered while they cook and expand. Taste and add more salt, if needed.

MAKE THE LAMB MERGUEZ

To grind the meat: Spread the lamb meat and pork fat out on a parchment paper–lined rimmed baking sheet. Freeze until the edges of the cubes are rigid but the middles are still pliable, about 30 minutes.

Meanwhile, toast the coriander, fennel, and cumin in a small, dry pan over medium heat for a few minutes, just until the fennel seeds begin turning golden brown.

Once the meat and fat are sufficiently cold, sprinkle the toasted spices, ground chile pepper, paprika, cayenne, and oregano over the meat and fat, then push the seasoned meat and fat along with the garlic cloves through a meat grinder fitted with a medium-fine die (3⁄16-inch/ 5-mm hole size). Alternatively, use a food processor fitted with a metal blade to grind the seasoned meat and fat along with the garlic, filling the bowl of the processor no more than halfway and working in batches.

Transfer the mixture to a large bowl. Mix in a few grinds of black pepper, the vinegar, and salt.

If you are using pre-ground lamb and finely chopped fat: Put them in a large bowl with all the seasonings. (You will need to first toast the coriander, fennel, and cumin as instructed and grind them using a mortar and pestle or a spice grinder. You will also need to mince the garlic before adding to the bowl.) Using your hands, mix everything together for a minute or two, until the meat has a tacky texture and the spices are well incorporated. Shape into 6 flattened football-shaped patties, each about 1 inch (2.5 cm) thick.

Heat a wide skillet over medium to medium-high heat for 1 minute. Swirl in enough oil to coat the bottom of the skillet, then add the patties. Sear until nicely caramelized on the first side, about 4 minutes. Flip them over and sear the second side just until the sausages are barely cooked through, with a nice pink core, another 4 minutes or so.

To serve, heat up the beans in their liquid. Add the roasted tomatoes and let them heat through. Spoon some beans and a few tomato pieces into each of six shallow bowls. Top with a cooked merguez sausage, breaking it into smaller pieces if you like. Dollop some labneh into each bowl, and garnish with mint.

Family Meal, Part 2, Windrose Farm

"Pozole" a la gringa

This is nothing like pozole. There's no pozole in this. However, it is quite good.

Serves 6 (GF)

1 pound (455 g) pork shoulder, cut into 2-inch (5-cm) pieces

Fine sea salt and freshly ground black pepper

1½ cups (180 g) shucked fresh beans, such as lima beans, black-eyed peas, or cranberry beans

2 tomatoes (4 ounces/115 g total)

5 cloves garlic

1 bay leaf

1 small dried chile pepper

Extra-virgin olive oil

½ yellow onion, diced, plus ¼ yellow onion

1 small poblano pepper or green bell pepper, stem and seeds removed, diced

1½ teaspoons ground coriander

1 teaspoon ground cumin

2 allspice berries

6 whole black peppercorns

2½ cups (340 g) husked tomatillos, halved

¼ bunch fresh cilantro, stemmed, plus more leaves for serving

1 lime, halved

Fresh amaranth leaves, basil leaves, and/or thinly sliced scallion

The day before you plan to cook, season the pork with 2 teaspoons salt and lots of black pepper. Cover and refrigerate overnight. (You can do this step a few hours ahead of time, but it's better if you let the meat rest overnight.)

The next day, put the shucked beans in a large pot and cover with 2 inches (5 cm) of cool water. Cut one of the tomatoes in half, squeeze both halves over the pot, then drop them into the water. Smash 2 of the garlic cloves and add them along with the bay leaf, chile, and 1 tea-spoon salt. Bring to a very gentle simmer. Cook until the beans are tender and creamy, 20 to 45 min-utes, depending on the bean. Taste and add a bit more salt, if needed. Drain the beans, reserving the cooking liquid.

Heat a large, heavy-bottomed pot over medium-high heat for 1 minute. Add enough oil to coat the bottom of the pot, then add half the sea-soned pork and cook until nicely browned on one side, 2 to 3 min-utes. Transfer the seared pork to a plate, then brown the other half and transfer it to the plate. Pour off all but about 2 tablespoons of the fat in the pot.

Reduce the heat to medium-low. Add the diced onion, poblano pep-per, and ½ teaspoon salt, and cook, stirring often, until the vegetables have softened, about 4 minutes.

While the vegetables soften, thinly slice 2 of the garlic cloves. Once the onion and pepper are ready, add the garlic to the pot and let sizzle for 1 minute. Stir in the coriander,

cumin, allspice, and peppercorns. Add the pork, the reserved bean cooking liquid, plus any additional water needed to cover the meat by 2 inches (5 cm). Bring to a slow simmer, cover the pot partially, and cook until the meat is falling-apart tender, about 2 hours.

Meanwhile, preheat the oven to 400°F (205°C).

Roast the tomatillos along with the remaining whole tomato, remain-ing 1 garlic clove, and ¼ onion on a rimmed baking sheet until collapsed and browned, about 25 minutes. Puree everything plus the cilantro in a blender or food processor, then transfer to a pot and simmer for 10 minutes. Season with lime juice and salt to taste.

Once the pork is tender, stir in the tomatillo sauce and the cooked beans. Simmer gently, stirring every so often, until the flavors have mingled, about 15 minutes. Taste, adding salt and lime juice as needed.

Serve with a garnish of amaranth, cilantro, basil, scallion, or all of the above.

NOTE ON BEANS

Dried beans can be substituted for the fresh shelling beans. Soak ½ cup (95 g) dried beans in plenty of water overnight before simmering them in the same amount of water and spices. Dried beans will take longer to cook—about 1 to 2 hours, sometimes even more. (If you're making the beans ahead of time, let them cool in their liquid.) Canned beans can also be substituted for the fresh ones. Rinse and drain one (15-ounce/430-g) can of beans, add to the pot with the water and other ingredients, and bring just to a simmer, then proceed with the recipe.

"Pozole" a la gringa

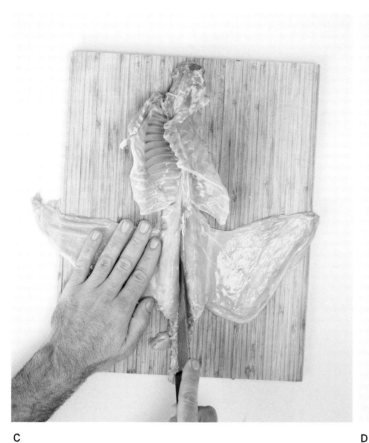

C

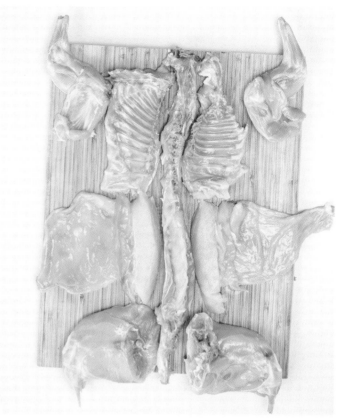

D

below the rib cage, cut across the left side, under the bottom rib, perpendicular to the spine. If you run into a rib bone, gracefully move around it. Stop cutting when you reach the spine. Turn the rabbit 180 degrees and make a similar cut on the tail end of the belly meat. Turn the rabbit again so that its tail is nearest to you. Now, focus! Removing the saddle is the trickiest part of rabbit fabrication. Cut directly along the left side of the spine, lifting and pulling the belly meat up away from the spine as you move the knife, until the left half of the belly meat is separated from the body. Repeat on the right side. You should now have two long belly meat pieces with no bones attached to them **(D)** (center) plus all the other parts of the rabbit.

Next, debone the forelegs: Hold the foot end of the leg and rest the other end on the cutting board. Starting at the top, cut downward, pressing the blade of your knife

very close to the bone in order to separate all the meat from the bone. Rotate the leg and repeat on all sides. It's okay to go back and cut off smaller bits of meat that stuck to the bone—all the foreleg meat will eventually be minced. Reserve all the bones.

MAKE THE RABBIT BALLOTINES

Set a large pan over medium heat and add the butter. Add the shallot, fennel, and carrot and cook, stirring occasionally, until tender but not browned, about 6 minutes. Add the caraway and green garlic and cook for another 2 to 3 minutes. Pour in the wine and let simmer until most of it has evaporated. Add the thyme, sage, and rosemary, then remove from the heat.

Mince the deboned foreleg meat and place it in a bowl. Place the upper loin meat in the bowl of a food proces-

E

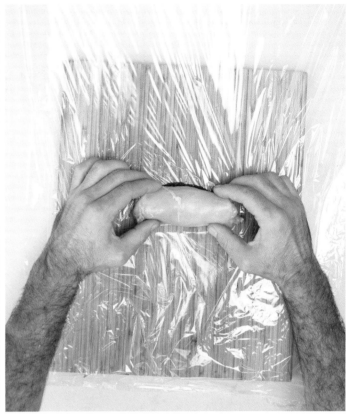

F

G

H

sor fitted with a metal blade. Cut each tenderloin piece lengthwise so that half remains attached to the belly flap. Add the loose halves to the bowl of the food processor. Add the egg and ½ cup (120 ml) of the cream. Process until smooth, stopping and scraping down the sides of the bowl as needed. Add the dill, parsley, greens, cooked vegetables, minced foreleg meat, lots of black pepper, and 1 teaspoon salt. Pulse a few times just to blend everything together. Gently shape a small patty, cook it in a pan, and taste to make sure there is enough salt. If not, add more and make another test.

Lay the belly pieces flat on a cutting board, arranging them so that the tenderloin piece is parallel to your shoulders. Season the bellies and tenderloins with salt. **(E)** Spread the processed meat mixture ⅜ inch (1 cm) thick across each belly flap. **(F)** Roll up each belly firmly but not so tightly that all the filling squirts out. **(G)** Wrap each in plastic as tightly as you can. **(H)** Poke each about a dozen times all over with a toothpick, then wrap in another piece of plastic.

Heat a large pot of water until it's barely simmering. Drop in the wrapped rabbit ballotines and poach them gently at a low simmer until they reach an internal temperature of 135°F (57°C), 15 to 20 minutes. Remove from the water and let cool completely. (The ballotines can be made up to this point and stored in the refrigerator for up to 3 days.)

MAKE THE RABBIT BONE BROTH

Place all the rabbit bones in a large pot. Add the onion, carrot, celery, peppercorns, bay leaf, thyme, and enough water to cover. Simmer for 5 hours. Strain, discarding the solids.

MAKE THE COLLARD BUNDLES

Preheat the oven to 300°F (150°C).

Place the hind legs in a single layer in a tall-sided baking dish or pot. Season them generously with salt and pepper. Add enough duck fat to cover completely. Add the garlic, bay leaf, thyme, rosemary, and peppercorns. Cover tightly, then place in the oven and bake until the meat is falling-off-the-bones tender, about 1 hour.

Let the legs cool in the fat, then pull all the meat off the bones. (Store the fat in an airtight container in the fridge for up to 6 months.) Raise the oven temperature to 350°F (175°C).

Blanch the collard leaves in boiling salted water until tender and bright green, then lay them out on a rimmed baking sheet and place in the fridge to cool. Trim off the thickest part of each stem, leaving most of each leaf intact. Take a small handful of the rabbit meat, gently squeeze it into a ball, and place it in the center of a collard leaf. Wrap the leaf up and around the meat to form a little bundle. If it seems easier, you can lay the leaves across a ladle or in a teacup and use the sloping sides to help you form the bundles. If the collards are really big, trim any excess that wraps around too much. Make six to eight bundles.

FINALLY (YOU MADE IT!), TO SERVE

Heat a cast-iron skillet over medium-high heat and add just enough oil to give the bottom of the pan a light sheen. Working in batches, unwrap the ballotines and sear the meat on all sides until golden brown. Transfer to a plate and let rest for 5 to 10 minutes.

Meanwhile, place the collard bundles in a baking dish with a splash of the rabbit bone broth and heat in the oven until warmed through.

Pour the remaining broth into a saucepan, bring to a boil, remove from the heat, and swirl in the butter. Stir in the green garlic puree and a squeeze of lemon juice, then taste and add a bit more salt, if needed.

Slice the ballotines into rounds ¾ inch (2 cm) thick and place a few slices in each of six to eight warmed shallow bowls. Place a warm collard bundle in each bowl. Pour the green garlic broth around the meat and collard bundle. Garnish with mustard greens, radishes, and celtuce. Finish with another squeeze of lemon juice and a pinch of fleur de sel.

GOT ANY EXTRA GREEN GARLIC PUREE?
Spread about 2 tablespoons on top of the processed meat filling.

Ramos-style short ribs and vegetables in beef consommé

Ramos-style short ribs and vegetables in beef consommé

Sqirl's chef-de-cuisine, Javier Ramos, came up with this rendition of his grandfather's favorite stew. The braising part of the recipe is simple in that it requires just plain water, not wine or broth. However, there's another step that comes next and makes this dish really special: The cooking liquid is fortified with beef broth, then clarified using a French technique. The resulting broth is rich but clear. As for the garnishes, if you can't find chayote, substitute kohlrabi or even celery.

Serves 6 (GF)

8 bay leaves
3 pounds (1.4 kg) beef short ribs
1 dried guajillo chile, coarsely ground
2 teaspoons freshly ground black pepper
Fine sea salt
Vegetable oil
2 cups (480 ml) beef stock, as needed
14 ounces (400 g) beef scrap (leftover meat odds and ends) or lean ground beef
½ large carrot, chopped

¼ small yellow onion, chopped
1 stalk celery, chopped
5 large egg whites
½ cup (25 g) purslane
¼ chayote, finely diced
1 handful squash blossoms, torn
6 small potatoes, boiled, peeled, and halved
½ lemon
Fleur de sel

Using tongs, hold the bay leaves one at a time over a gas flame, turning and toasting them for a few seconds. Crumble the toasted leaves with your hands.

Season the short ribs on all sides with the bay, chile, black pepper, and 1 tablespoon salt. Cover and let rest in the refrigerator for at least 3 hours and up to 24 hours.

Take the short ribs out of the fridge to temper at room temperature for at least 1 hour. About 10 minutes before you're ready to cook, preheat the oven to 300°F (150°C).

Set a cast-iron pan over medium-high heat. Add enough oil to coat the bottom of the pan. Working in batches, sear the short ribs, turning until deeply browned on all sides, about 10 minutes per batch. You don't want to crowd the meat in the pan or it won't brown properly. If the bits of meat stuck to the pan start looking too dark, add a splash of water to prevent burning.

Transfer the browned short ribs to a Dutch oven or roasting pan with tall sides. Pour about ½ cup (120 ml) water into the hot pan to deglaze it, using a wooden spoon to scrape up the stuck bits from the bottom and sides of the pan. Pour this flavorful deglazing liquid over the short ribs, then add enough water to come three-quarters of the way up the ribs. Cover the Dutch oven tightly with a lid or a makeshift lid made of aluminum foil and place in the oven to braise until the meat is completely tender, 2 to 2½ hours.

Transfer the meat to a plate and pour all the liquid into a large glass measuring cup (or two). Let settle for a few minutes, then skim off most of the fat that has risen to the surface. There should be about 4 cups (960 ml). Return the cooking liquid to the pot and add enough beef stock to make about 6 cups (1.4 L) total.

Using a food processor, blend the beef scrap, carrot, onion, celery, and egg whites until finely chopped and well combined. Add this mixture to the saucepan. Slowly bring the stock to a simmer over medium-low heat, stirring frequently. It looks a little crazy at this point but stay with me. Once the egg-white mixture forms a foamy raft on the surface, stop stirring and let simmer gently for 30 to 45 minutes, until the broth beneath the foam is clear.

Tip the pot slightly to shift the foam to one side and ladle the broth through a fine-mesh sieve into a clean pot, discarding the raft. Season the broth with salt.

To serve, place 1 or 2 short ribs in each of six bowls. Arrange the purslane, chayote, squash blossoms, and potatoes beautifully around the

meat. Heat the broth until it is piping hot, then ladle it into the bowls. Finish with a squeeze of lemon juice and a sprinkle of fleur de sel.

NOTE ON VEGETABLES FOR SERVING
We used spinach and pickled red onion (page 146) here; you can really use any vegetables you like.

A

A. Jayme Darling lifting weights
B. Edgar Rico realizes it's the end of service
C. Javier Ramos tasting as he goes
D. Mike Lockward adds the lunch specials
E. David Prado's pro-porridge moves

B

C

D

E

A

B

C

D

E

F

A. Meadow Ramsey is on quiche patrol
B. Magdiel Ulloa scales up
C. Sqirl After Hours
D. Tonye Dunn means biscuits
E. Ethan Weiner stocks up
F. Herbage

Party on, Wayne Rambharose

Fish
152—175

When you think of fish for breakfast, you likely imagine lox. For dinner, maybe a grilled fillet over a bed of wilted greens and grains. These are great classics to rely on. But what about the range that fish can offer? In this chapter you will find a recipe for our version of lox, but you'll also find recipes for a number of fish dishes that can be served more as snacks or starter courses. Most people automatically serve fish as the centerpiece of a meal, but sometimes it's nice to try something different. There's no right way to eat fish. And if you do happen to prefer cooking a fish fillet, I've included an option for that as well.

Salmon with sorrel pesto

Salmon with sorrel pesto

When I first tasted the classic Troisgros combination of salmon and sorrel, I remember thinking about how beautifully the bright acidity of the sorrel played against the richness of the salmon. Then my next thought was, "How can I make a dish with sorrel that is completely different?" Sqirl's sorrel pesto–topped rice bowl came about because of that desire. And now here I am, returning full circle, putting our sorrel pesto on simply prepared fillets of salmon. Life is funny that way.

Serves 2 (GF)

2 (6-ounce/170-g) salmon fillets, skin-on
Fine sea salt and freshly ground black pepper
2 tablespoons extra-virgin olive oil
2 tablespoons unsalted butter
2 big handfuls (2 ounces/55 g total) sorrel,
    stemmed
¼ cup (60 ml) Sorrel Pesto (page 63)
½ lemon
Fleur de sel

Preheat the oven to 350°F (175°C).

Generously season the salmon with salt and pepper on both sides. Heat a large oven-safe pan over medium-high heat for 1 minute. Add the olive oil and butter. Once the butter has melted completely, place the fish, skin-side down, in the pan. Cook, without moving the fish, until the skin is crisp and nicely browned, about 5 minutes. Transfer the pan to the oven (do not flip the salmon) and roast until the fish is cooked to your desired doneness, 3 to 4 minutes for medium-rare.

Arrange the sorrel leaves in the center of two plates. Place the salmon on top of the sorrel. The leaves will begin to wilt from the residual heat. Spoon the sorrel pesto over the fish and finish with a big squeeze of lemon juice and a pinch of fleur de sel.

Stone crab fried rice with its mustard and kumquat

Stone crab fried rice with its mustard and kumquat

If you've never tasted the "mustard" inside a crab, you are in for a treat. It's the mustard of the sea, and here it is used to flavor fried rice. We sometimes serve the rice in the hollowed-out crab shells, and I like to think of them as drought-tolerant plateware.

Serves 4 to 6 (GF)

2 cloves garlic, smashed
½ cup plus 3 tablespoons (165 ml) soy sauce
4 live stone crabs
2 cups (400 g) short-grain brown or white rice
3 tablespoons vegetable oil
1 tablespoon fish sauce
3 large eggs, beaten
Leaves from ½ bunch fresh cilantro, chopped
Leaves from ½ bunch fresh mint, chopped

½ jalapeño, seeded and finely chopped
3 scallions, thinly sliced
1 cup (140 g) kumquats, sliced and seeded
¼ cup (60 ml) hot sauce (page 267 or store-bought)
Garlic chips (page 100; optional)
2 or 3 limes, halved
Fleur de sel

Bring a large pot of water to a boil. Add the garlic and ½ cup (120 ml) of the soy sauce. Drop in the live crabs and let them simmer for 10 minutes.

Transfer the crabs to a plate and let cool. Save the cooking liquid.

Discard about half the crab-cooking liquid and top up the pot with fresh water. Bring to a simmer, then add the rice and cook until tender, about 30 minutes.

Drain and let cool completely. All the way. Cold and dry. Frying warm rice is tricky—it's tough not to end up with a gluey final product.

While the rice cools, pick the crab-meat out of the shells: Crack the legs and pull out the meat. Open up the body by pulling the top shell away from the bottom shell. There's a little tab on the underside rear-end, and if you pull it, you'll expose a little gap that'll help you to lift the top shell off. Inside near the head you'll find some yellow-brown goo. Scoop this out and keep it! It's the crab's mustard, also called the *hepatopancreas*, which is a fun word and a delicious thing. Pick out any meat from the body. Some stone crabs are too small and there won't be much body meat. Set all the crabmeat aside.

Set a large skillet over medium-high heat. Add the oil and the cooled rice and leave it alone for a moment until it begins to brown. Stir, then leave it alone again. Repeat the stirring and leaving-alone process several more times, until there are lots of crunchy, browned bits of rice. Pour in the remaining 3 tablespoons soy sauce along with the fish sauce. Add the crabmeat and eggs and stir well. Once the crab has heated through and the eggs have scrambled, remove from the heat and mix in the cilantro, mint, jalapeño, scallions, kumquats, and hot sauce.

Serve the fried rice garnished with garlic chips, plenty of lime juice, fleur de sel, and a dollop of the crab mustard.

SHORTCUTS
You can make this with day-old cooked rice (takeout leftovers are ideal) and 8 ounces (225 g) lump crabmeat.

Squid toast

I love watching the faces of customers as they receive a piece of our baguette toast, which we typically cut from tip to tip instead of crosswise. Hugh Acheson calls it "the big crouton," and this recipe might be the sexiest application for the toast.

Serves 4 to 6

6 small or 3 medium tomatoes (1 pound/455 g total)

¼ cup (60 ml) plus 3 tablespoons extra-virgin olive oil, plus more for brushing

Leaves from 3 sprigs resinous herbs (such as thyme, rosemary, sage, or savory)

3 cloves garlic

Fine sea salt

1 pound (455 g) cleaned squid bodies and tentacles, patted dry

1 teaspoon ground cumin

1 teaspoon ground coriander

1 teaspoon fennel seeds

1 lemon, zested and halved

1 baguette

¾ cup (120 g) aioli (page 263)

½ cup (20 g) fresh soft herbs (such as basil, chervil, parsley, mint, cilantro, dill, and chives), chopped

Fleur de sel

MAKE THE SLOW-ROASTED TOMATOES

Preheat the oven to 250°F (120°C).

Remove any stems from the tomatoes and cut out any tough cores. If the tomatoes are small, cut them in half through their equators. If they are medium, cut them in half through their equators and then cut each half into two or three wedges. Lay them skin-side down on a rimmed baking sheet. In a small pot over low heat, warm ¼ cup (60 ml) of the oil, herb sprigs, and 1 garlic clove for a moment, just until the oil is infused with the garlic and herb flavors. Brush the cut sides of the tomatoes with the infused oil, reserving the remaining oil. Lightly season each wedge with a pinch of salt. Roast until concentrated,

collapsed, and slightly browned, 1 to 2 hours. (Roasted tomatoes can be made ahead and stored in the infused oil, covered, in the refrigerator for up to 3 days.)

Place the squid in a bowl, add the cumin, coriander, fennel, the grated zest of the lemon, and 1 tablespoon of the oil, and toss well. Let marinate for 15 minutes.

Preheat the oven to 325°F (165°C).

Using a long serrated knife, cut the baguette in half lengthwise (yes, you read that right—lengthwise!). Brush with oil, then toast in the oven directly on the rack until crisp, about 8 minutes. As soon as you pull the toasts out of the oven, rub them with the remaining garlic. Sprinkle with salt and set aside.

Heat a large cast-iron skillet over medium-high heat and add the remaining 2 tablespoons oil. Season the marinated squid with ½ teaspoon salt. Working in batches, sear the squid in the pan until all sides are lightly browned and the biggest pieces are opaque all the way through, 3 to 4 minutes; cut into the biggest piece to make sure it's not goopy on the inside. Transfer the cooked squid to a bowl and continue searing the rest. Toss all the cooked squid with the slow-roasted tomatoes.

Spread the aioli thickly across the baguette toasts. Spoon the squid and tomatoes over the top. Garnish with the soft herbs, a pinch of fleur de sel, and a squeeze of juice from the zested lemon.

Grilled ridgeback prawns with piri piri sauce

Ridgeback prawns are readily available in Southern California. They're sweet and tender but difficult to peel. They're also quite small. If you can't find them where you are, substitute spot prawns or large shrimp. Here we serve them with our rendition of piri piri sauce, which is much less spicy than the traditional version.

Serves 6 as a first course or 4 as a main (GF)

FOR THE PRAWNS

36 ridgeback prawns (or spot prawns, or 24 large shrimp)
2 tablespoons chopped fresh tarragon
2 tablespoons chopped fresh parsley
1 tablespoon chopped fresh oregano or marjoram, or 1 teaspoon dried oregano or marjoram
2 cloves garlic, minced
Grated zest of 1 orange
¼ cup (60 ml) extra-virgin olive oil
Fine sea salt and freshly ground black pepper

FOR THE PIRI PIRI SAUCE

2 tablespoons extra-virgin olive oil
3 cloves garlic
½ yellow onion, chopped
1 teaspoon fresh thyme leaves
Pinch of cayenne, plus more if desired
10 canned piquillo peppers, liquid reserved
2 tablespoons fresh lemon juice
¼ cup (60 ml) red wine vinegar
Fine sea salt

TO SERVE

½ lemon
Fleur de sel

PREPARE THE PRAWNS

First pull off the heads. (These can be tossed in rice flour and fried in canola oil heated to 350°F/175°C. Once crispy, transfer to a plate and sprinkle with salt and ground chile—a cook's snack!) Remove the outer shell and legs, keeping the tail and inner shell intact. On the underside/belly of each prawn, make two small cuts perpendicular to the length of the prawn, then press gently to flatten. This step will help prevent the prawns from curling and tightening up when they cook, but it is purely for aesthetic reasons and can be omitted.

Thread 3 prawns (or 2 shrimp, if you're using shrimp) onto one bamboo skewer, poking the skewer from the tail end of each prawn through the body toward the head. Repeat with the remaining prawns, for 12 skewers total.

In a bowl, stir together the tarragon, parsley, oregano, garlic, orange zest, and oil. Season the skewered prawns with salt and black pepper, then rub the herby marinade all over them and set aside at room temperature for 30 minutes.

Preheat the grill.

MAKE THE PIRI PIRI SAUCE

Heat a large pan over medium-low heat. Add the olive oil, garlic, onion, thyme, and cayenne. Cook, stirring often, until the vegetables have softened, about 4 minutes. Transfer to a blender and add the piquillo peppers, lemon juice, and vinegar. Blend until very smooth, adding a splash of the canned pepper liquid if needed to get the mixture moving. Season with salt. You can also add a bit more cayenne, if you're craving more heat.

When you're ready to cook the prawns, grill them over high heat, turning once or twice, until lightly charred and just cooked through, about 5 minutes. Alternatively, cook them under the broiler, turning often. Squeeze some lemon juice over the cooked prawns, sprinkle with fleur de sel, and serve with the piri piri sauce.

Fried sturgeon with tartar sauce

Welcome to my childhood. When Patch, a chef here at Sqirl, introduced me to the idea of using sturgeon instead of cod for fish and chips, I was floored. Sturgeon, it turns out, is a fish that holds up well to frying, retaining a delicate texture under fryer-y circumstances. We use sustainably farmed sturgeon from California's Passmore Ranch, which makes the use of this fish even more interesting to me. If sturgeon is hard to find, look for sustainably sourced cod. This fish and chips dish comes sans chips, but feel free to add them if you want.

Serves 6

FOR THE TARTAR SAUCE

½ cup (120 g) crème fraîche (page 265 or store-bought) or sour cream
½ cup (115 g) aioli (page 263) or mayonnaise
2 tablespoons finely chopped preserved Meyer lemon rind (page 64)
2 tablespoons fresh lemon juice
2 tablespoons finely diced cucumber pickle (we like to use the lactofermented kind; Bubbies Pure Kosher Dills are great)
½ bunch fresh dill, chopped
Freshly ground black pepper and fine sea salt

FOR THE FRIED STURGEON

Vegetable oil, for frying (about 4 cups/960 ml)
1 cup (125 g) all-purpose flour
2 large eggs
½ cup (120 ml) heavy cream
2 cups (120 g) panko bread crumbs (or leftover brioche, crust removed, ground in a food processor and toasted until crunchy)
6 (4-ounce/115-g) sturgeon fillets, skin and bones removed
Fine sea salt and freshly ground black pepper
Fleur de sel
Lemon wedges

MAKE THE TARTAR SAUCE

It's a one-bowl, one-step process. You got this. Mix together the crème fraîche, aioli, preserved lemon, lemon juice, pickle, dill, and a few grinds of pepper. Taste and season with a bit of salt, if needed, depending on how salty the preserved lemon and pickles are. (You can make the sauce up to 4 days ahead of time and store, covered, in the refrigerator.)

MAKE THE FRIED STURGEON

Set a large cast-iron skillet over medium-high heat and pour in enough oil to fill the skillet halfway.

While the oil heats, set up three bowls in a row. The flour goes in the first bowl. Beat the eggs and cream together in the second bowl until well combined and pale yellow in color. The panko goes in the third bowl. Line a plate with paper towels or a brown grocery bag.

Season the sturgeon fillets with salt and pepper on all sides. Working one at a time, drop a fillet in the first bowl and turn to coat it completely in flour. Move it to the second bowl for an eggy dunk, then place it in the third bowl and gently press the panko on all sides. The sturgeon is now ready to be fried in the hot oil.

To test if the oil is hot enough and ready, drop a few panko crumbs into it—they should do nothing for a split second and then begin to sizzle. If they sizzle right away and begin to burn, the oil is too hot. If they don't sizzle at all, it's too cold.

You can probably fit four fillets in the pan at a time; try not to crowd them. Fry, flipping often, until deep golden brown and cooked through, about 3 minutes. You may need to adjust the heat under the skillet to keep the oil at the right temperature because it'll cool down a little when you add the fish.

Transfer the sturgeon to the paper towels. Sprinkle generously with fleur de sel and serve with the tartar sauce for dipping and lemon wedges for squeezing.

Baccalà flower pot

Baccalà flower pot
local ling cod, crunchy quinoa, and herbs

While salt cod is an important and beautiful way we can preserve fish, I can also say that in its off-white spread form, it is just not the Emily Ratajkowski of fish dishes. However, packed into a jar and topped with crunchy quinoa, herbs, and flowers, it becomes a visually appealing thing.

Remember those flower pots we made as kids? The ones with chocolate pudding, Oreo crumbs, and gummy worms? Well, this is sort of like the savory, grown-up version. My favorite way to present this dish is to place a jar at each table setting, scatter toast in the center of the table, and let people start eating a shared meal.

Serves 6

FOR THE CRUNCHY QUINOA

¼ cup (45 g) red quinoa
Fine sea salt

FOR THE LING COD

1 pound (455 g) ling cod fillets, bones and skin removed
½ cup (70 g) kosher salt or coarse sea salt
1 large russet potato
1 cup (240 ml) whole milk
1 bay leaf
3 sprigs fresh thyme
6 whole black peppercorns
½ cup (120 ml) crème fraîche (page 265 or store-bought)
1 clove garlic, minced
Freshly ground black pepper
½ cup (120 ml) extra-virgin olive oil
Fine sea salt

TO SERVE

¼ cup (13 g) fresh soft herb leaves (such as chervil, dill, and parsley)
Edible flowers (optional)
Country-style bread, toasted

MAKE THE CRUNCHY QUINOA

Preheat the oven to 225°F (110°C).

Cook the quinoa in salted boiling water until tender, about 15 minutes. Drain, then spread the quinoa out on a rimmed baking sheet. Toast in the oven, stirring a few times, until crunchy, 15 to 20 minutes.

(Store in an airtight container for up to 3 months. It's sort of like granola; it might get a little moist after a little while, but just pop it back into the oven until it's crunchy again.)

MAKE THE LING COD

Measure the thickness of the fillet (in inches) and make a note of it somewhere.

Spread the kosher salt out on a plate. Set the fish on top of the salt and press down gently. Flip the fish and press again. Keep flipping and pressing until the fish is well coated in salt and there isn't much salt left on the plate.

Wrap the salted fish in cheesecloth, place it on a rack set over a rimmed baking sheet to catch drips, and place in the refrigerator. Use the following equation to figure out how long the fish needs to stay in the fridge:

$$\text{inches thick} \times 24 = \text{hours in fridge}$$

So if your fish is 1¼ inch (3.2 cm) thick, it will be in the fridge for 30 hours. While the fish is in the fridge, flip it over every 6 hours or however often you can remember to do it. Once it's done, unwrap the fish, rinse well, and pat dry. Wrap it up again in a fresh piece of cheese-

cloth, place it on the rack and back into the fridge for 5 days. (At this point, it can be stored in the fridge for up to 1 month.)

To use the salt cod, first you'll need to soak it: Submerge it in a bowl of cool water for 24 hours, changing the water every 6 hours or so.

When you're ready to make the flower pots, preheat the oven to 350°F (175°C). Wrap the potato in aluminum foil and bake it until tender, about 1 hour. Leave the oven on.

Meanwhile, in a saucepan or small pot set over medium heat, warm the milk until it's just barely steaming. Add the bay leaf, thyme, and peppercorns, then lower the soaked salt cod into the milk. Cook gently over low heat until the fish is tender and flaky, 5 to 7 minutes. It should be opaque all the way through, but make sure not to overcook it or it'll be tough.

Once the potato is done, cut it in half lengthwise and use a spoon to scoop all the flesh into a bowl, leav-

ing the potato skin for some other purpose. (I like to fry it in a little olive oil until crisp!) Add the cooked fish to the bowl along with the crème fraîche, garlic, a few grinds of pepper, and ¼ cup (60 ml) of the oil. Using a rubber spatula, mix everything together, gently breaking up the fish and potato into small flakes. Mix in the remaining ¼ cup (60 ml) oil, then taste and add salt, only if needed.

Spoon the baccalà into six small oven-safe vessels. (We use jam jars.) Pop them into the oven (350°F/175°C is fine; it doesn't really matter) to heat through and brown a little bit on the top. Remove from the oven, scatter the crunchy quinoa on top, and garnish with the herbs and flowers and other pretty things. Serve with toast.

DON'T WANT TO BOTHER WITH MAKING YOUR OWN SALT COD?

You can definitely buy salt cod from your nearest and most respectable seafood store or deli. It may need to be soaked for a little more time or a little less time, depending on how salty it is.

Baccalà flower pot

Royston Garza's gone fishing

Pickled sardine mezze platter

Sardines are fish that pickle really well—they retain their shape nicely.
If you don't feel like pickling fish, you could substitute store-bought smoked trout
or make Beet-Cured Salmon (page 175).

Serves 6 to 8 for snacks (GFO)

1 tablespoon coriander seeds
1 tablespoon fennel seeds
1 tablespoon yellow mustard seeds
12 whole black peppercorns
1 star anise
Pinch of dried chile pepper flakes
2 small shallots, thinly sliced
1 bay leaf
1 cup (240 ml) apple cider vinegar
1 cup (240 ml) white wine
2 tablespoons sugar

¼ cup (40 g) fine sea salt
8 to 10 filleted skin-on fresh sardines

TO SERVE

8 slices *rugbrød* or dark rye bread
1 cup Kohlrabi Tzatziki (recipe follows)
½ cup (75 g) Quick-Pickled Red Onions (recipe
  follows), drained
3 or 4 soft-boiled eggs (page 22), peeled and
  halved

In a small, dry pot set over medium-low heat, toast the coriander, fennel, mustard seeds, peppercorns, and star anise until fragrant, about 4 minutes. Add the pepper flakes, shallot, bay leaf, vinegar, and wine and bring to a simmer. Cook for 5 to 7 minutes, then add the sugar and salt, stirring until dissolved. Remove from the heat and let cool completely.

Lay the sardines in a shallow dish and pour the cooled brine over them. Cover, place in the refrigerator, and let pickle overnight.

Serve the pickled sardines on a large platter with the *rugbrød*, kohlrabi tzatziki, pickled onions, and soft-boiled eggs.

NOTE

It's fun and a little unexpected to serve this with dehydrated capers. To make them, rinse salt-packed or brined capers, then spread them out on a rimmed baking sheet. Place in an oven set to the lowest possible setting (200°F/90°C for most ovens) to dehydrate for 8 to 12 hours, until dried and crisp.

Kohlrabi tzatziki

Not just for pickled sardine mezze platters, this is delicious with chicken and rice. You could also put a dollop on a roasted purple yam à la the loaded sweet potato at Superiority Burger.

Makes 1 cup (230 g)

1 cup (240 g) whole-milk yogurt
2 small or 1 medium kohlrabi, tops removed
    (300 g total)
Fine sea salt
¼ teaspoon ground cumin
¼ teaspoon coriander seeds, toasted and
    ground
¼ Preserved Meyer Lemon, inner flesh scraped off,
    rind finely chopped (page 64 or store-bought)
Freshly ground black pepper

Pickled sardine mezze platter

First, you'll need to strain both the yogurt and the kohlrabi separately for 24 hours. To do so, set up a couple of straining stations: Line two colanders with cheesecloth, then set each in a bowl that's big enough for the colander to hover above the bottom of the bowl.

Pour the yogurt into one and let strain in the fridge for 24 hours.

Peel the kohlrabi and cut it into big chunks. Using a food processor, pulse until the kohlrabi is very finely chopped and resembles gravel. Alternatively, grate on the largest holes of a box grater. Mix the kohlrabi with 1 teaspoon salt, then transfer to the second straining station and let strain in the fridge for 24 hours.

On the following day, squeeze the kohlrabi to wring out any last liquid. Discard the kohlrabi liquid and keep the whey that dripped from the yogurt.

In a bowl, mix together the strained yogurt, strained kohlrabi, cumin, coriander, and preserved lemon rind. Taste, adding pepper and a bit more salt if needed. If you'd like the tzatziki to be thinner, just stir in a splash of the reserved whey.

Store, covered, in the refrigerator for up to 3 days.

Quick-pickled red onions

Try adding a few of these to the Roasted Chicken Salad (page 123) or try on tacos!

Makes about 3 cups (840 g)

1½ cups (360 ml) red wine vinegar
⅓ cup (65 g) sugar
1 teaspoon fine sea salt
3 large red onions (1 pound/455 g total), sliced
   ⅛ inch (3 mm) thick
1½ teaspoons juniper berries
¾ teaspoon cumin seeds
¾ teaspoon coriander seeds
1 bay leaf

Combine the vinegar, sugar, and salt in a small pot. Heat, stirring until the sugar has dissolved completely. Remove from the heat.

Bring a large pot of water to a boil. Drop in the onions and cook for 1 minute. Using a slotted spoon, transfer the onions to a bowl.

Add the juniper, cumin, coriander, and bay leaf to the bowl with the onions. Pour in the vinegar mixture, cover, and place in the refrigerator to chill until cold.

The pickled onions will keep, covered, in the refrigerator for several weeks.

Black cod ceviche
with purple yam and aguachile

Served hot, black cod should be cooked all the way through. In this ceviche dish, we leave the raw fish to "cook" in citrus juice for an hour or two. It's a long time, but it's worth it. The sweetness from the purple yams is a nice addition, although they aren't necessary and you can leave them out if you feel like it.

Serves 6 (GF)

FOR THE CEVICHE

1 pound (455 g) absolutely fresh black cod
  fillets, skin and bones removed
2 teaspoons fine sea salt
¼ cup (60 ml) fresh lemon juice
3 tablespoons fresh lime juice

FOR THE PURPLE YAMS

3 or 4 small Japanese purple yams
  (17 ounces/500 g total), scrubbed
Extra-virgin olive oil
Fine sea salt and freshly ground black pepper

FOR THE AGUACHILE

6 large ripe red tomatoes (2 pounds 14 ounces/
  1.3 kg total), stems removed, quartered
1 or 2 serrano chiles, seeded
2 cloves garlic
1 tablespoon sherry vinegar
2 tablespoons fresh lime juice
1 teaspoon fine sea salt

TO SERVE

Cilantro pistou (page 71)
Leaves from 6 sprigs fresh cilantro
Leaves from 6 sprigs fresh parsley
Tortilla chips (optional)

MAKE THE CEVICHE

Using a super-sharp knife, cut the black cod against the grain into slices ½ inch (6 mm) thick, then cut the slices into cubes. Place in a wide, shallow container. Sprinkle with the salt, toss well, and let rest in the fridge for 30 minutes.

When the fish is ready, pour the lemon and lime juices over the top and toss well. Let rest once again in the fridge, stirring every 20 minutes or so, until the fish becomes firm and opaque, 1 to 2 hours.

MAKE THE PURPLE YAMS

Preheat the oven to 350°F (175°C).

Rub the yams with a bit of oil, sprinkle with salt and pepper, and wrap individually in aluminum foil. Put on a baking sheet and roast until they can be easily pierced with a fork, 40 to 60 minutes, depending on their size. (If the yams are different sizes, remove each one as it is done.) Purple yams can be cooked ahead of time and stored in the refrigerator for several days.

MEANWHILE, MAKE THE AGUACHILE

Blend the tomato, chile, garlic, vinegar, lime juice, and salt in a blender. Strain through a nut-milk bag for a very smooth result or through a fine-mesh sieve for a slightly less smooth but no less delicious result. If you use a nut-milk bag, you may want to wear plastic gloves to squeeze out the liquid because the chile can irritate your hands; discard the solids. Taste and adjust the seasoning, adding more salt if needed. Set aside at room temperature.

TO SERVE

Cut the purple yams into slices about ¼ inch (6 mm) thick and arrange a few of them in each of six shallow bowls. Divide the fish among the bowls, then spoon in enough aguachile to cover the bottom of each bowl. Drizzle a little pistou over the top and garnish with the herbs. Serve with chips, if you like.

Beet-cured salmon

Beet-cured salmon

Not just for bagels.

Makes 1 side of salmon (about 1 pound 10 ounces/740 g) (GF)

2 red beets (8 ounces/225 g total)
1 cup (140 g) coarse sea salt or kosher salt
½ cup (100 g) sugar
1-inch (2.5-cm) piece of ginger, peeled and
    chopped
Grated zest of 1 lemon
½ bunch fresh dill
2 teaspoons dill seeds

2 teaspoons coriander seeds
2 teaspoons whole black peppercorns
4 allspice berries
4 juniper berries
Pinch of ground cinnamon
Pinch of freshly grated nutmeg
1 whole skin-on side of salmon (about
    2 pounds/910 g total), scaled

Peel the beets, chop them into pieces, then pulverize in the bowl of a food processor fitted with a metal blade. Add the salt, sugar, ginger, lemon zest, fresh dill, dill seeds, coriander, peppercorns, allspice, juniper, cinnamon, and nutmeg. Process to combine.

Fully cured salmon after the fridge

Place the salmon skin-side down on a rimmed baking sheet. Use your fingers to feel for and remove any pin bones. Take about half the beet cure and press it into the salmon, covering the top completely but getting most of the cure on the thickest part of the fish. Cover with a large piece of plastic wrap, then flip the salmon over and press the remaining beet cure into the other side. Wrap the fish tightly in the plastic, then set another baking sheet on top of the salmon and weigh it down with a couple of cans of tomatoes or something similar. Pop the whole thing in the fridge and let cure for 24 hours, until the salmon feels firm but not rock hard and not mushy, either. While it cures, the salmon will lose some water weight and the liquid might pool in the baking sheet.

Not a huge deal, just something good to know.

Rinse the salmon with cool water, gently brushing off the beet cure, then blot dry.

To slice, hold your knife at a 45-degree angle in relation to the cutting board and cut the salmon into slices as thin as possible, starting at the tail end and moving toward the thicker end, leaving the skin behind.

Beet-cured salmon can be stored in the refrigerator for up to 2 weeks.

NOTE ON SPICES
Think of the spices called for in this recipe as guidelines and don't be afraid to substitute your favorite spices (or those you have on hand).

This chapter is dedicated to the inimitable Ron Cornelsen

Shady Lady

Jessica Koslow's Not Very Sweet Yet Totally Unsavory Rise to Stardom

If you went to court while under the age of eighteen for doing something wrong, you may be able to get the record sealed. This includes records held by law enforcement, the district attorney, probation, and the courts. When the court orders your records sealed, it means that the offense that brought you to court no longer exists by law, and you can legally and truthfully say you do not have a criminal record when asked about your criminal history (there may be an exception to this if you want to join the military or get a federal security clearance).
According to the Judicial Branch of the State of California

EDITOR'S NOTE: The juvenile criminal court records of Jessica Anne Effron Koslow were, in fact, sealed by the State of California. However, when Koslow applied to the United States Armed Forces to go to Afghanistan and cook for the troops during the 2015 Christmas season, they were unsealed to the military. A member of the United States Special Operations Forces—an Army Delta Force operator—legally provided these court documents to Krikorian Writes. They are the basis for much of the following report.

If you are among the devotees of Jessica Koslow—and her intense dose of Los Angeles known as Sqirl—then you know "The Line."

If you are not, then be informed that "The Line" is what you will get in when you come to Sqirl. It's not merely a waiting line. It is Act One of the Sqirl experience. Sqirl without the line, well, it just wouldn't be as good. Then again, Sqirl without the line is not going to happen.

Customers talk to other customers in that line. They share their latest personal stories. They gossip. They might talk about Jonathan Gold's latest review or who has been nominated from town for the James Beard Awards. There'll be Laker and Dodger talk. They might even talk politics. But what they don't talk about is the criminal past of Jessica Koslow. They don't talk about that because, until now, no one except Jessica, her parents, the judge, the district attorney's office, and her victims even knew about it.

Until now. So, folks in "The Line," here's a li'l somethin' to talk about next time you head to Virgil Avenue and Marathon Street for some Moro blood orange with vanilla bean marmalade.

Jessica's first years on Earth—in Long Beach, California—were crime-free. It was when she moved on to the exclusive Chadwick School in Palos Verdes that the trouble began.

Dr. Jayme Darling, professor of juvenile criminal behavioral studies at Stanford University, said that the transition from a working-class neighborhood such as Long Beach to an affluent community, such as Palos Verdes is often a grueling change for a child.

"A kid like Jessica from the rough-and-tumble streets of Long Beach suddenly transported to an elite school in Palos Verdes, well, it's no surprise she started getting into trouble," Darling said. "Here's a tough street kid who is accustomed to throwing—and taking—a punch, and now she's around spoiled kids who are scared shitless by a mere threat."

A spokesperson for Sqirl, Sara Storrie, declined to comment on Dr. Darling's theory other than to say, "The Stanford lady professor is generalizing, and at Sqirl that's not a good thing."

Regardless, according to the court records and verified by a former vice principal at Chadwick, Koslow punched a boy in the nose in the fifth grade after she misunderstood something he had said.

The following is a school report on the incident:

A boy [name redacted] was making fun of a girl's bra and said, "Michelle's bra is stupid." Jessica Koslow, without any warning, punched him on the nose, causing mild bleeding. Later, Koslow said she thought the boy had said "Michel Bras is stupid." It was later confirmed that Michel Bras is a renowned French chef with a legendary restaurant in the town of Laguiole, France, and a hero of Koslow's. When this was confirmed, authorities, knowing Laguiole is famous for its knives, obtained a search warrant and found twenty-nine very sharp steak knives in Jessica's underwear drawer. Counseling was ordered.

But the incident that put Koslow in handcuffs happened when she was in the tenth grade. A twelfth grade boy, whose name is protected by the Child Victims Act of 2002, was, according to several eyewitnesses, bullying a group of ninth- and tenth-graders. Right before he would push, kick, or punch them, he yelled out, in a very pronounced, exaggerated fashion "I, I, I am going to harm you!"

Observing this, and about to peel a Moro blood orange, was Jessica. As the bully repeated his threat, yelling out the second "I"—with his mouth wide open—Koslow fired the blood orange his way. Now this blood orange must've been guided by the left arm of Sandy Koufax as it went directly into the boy's agape mouth. It was thrown with such force that not only did it enter the mouth; it lodged in the soft *palate*. The boy immediately began choking.

As the students looked on in a mix of horror and celebration, Koslow calmly walked over and kicked the boy in the back of his neck.

This is where the controversy ensued.

As a result of the kick, the boy hurled the blood orange and was able to breathe. However, the Los Angeles District Attorney's Office, after a thorough review, said the kick "was not designed to help the boy, but rather to inflict great bodily injury."

(A full report can be seen at www.LACITY.ORG/KOSLOWKICK/ CHADWICK.)

After a brief trial, Koslow was sent to the infamous Los Padrinos Juvenile Hall in Downey.

It was here, in one of America's most notorious juvenile facilities, that Jessica Koslow's career began.

A brief introduction to the facility is in order. Unlike, say, at San Quentin or Folsom, the cells here had windows. They were barred and tiny. A human could not crawl through but still they were windows.

It just so happened that Koslow's windows were near a fruit orchard where trees were weighed down with Meyer lemons and Moro blood oranges. There were also exceedingly tall brambles—from neglect— with blackberries and raspberries.

One night, as she read *Crime and Punishment* on her threadbare cot, a lone Meyer lemon and a branch of blackberries blew into her cell on a summer breeze. As she was immersed in the anguish of Rodion Raskolnikov, she absentmindedly grabbed the fruit and, with all her fury, squeezed. A few minutes later—that book always does this to Jessica, to this day— she was asleep.

In the morning, the jail guard abruptly opened her cell door and slid in the daily

180

prison-style "breakfast" of bread and water. As she sat up in that measly cot, she noticed the smashed fruit—the Meyer lemon and blackberries—in a rather pretty clump on the floor.

With an elegant movement, she swooped the fruit up with the jailhouse bread and took a bite.

Do you know the opening lines to Irving Berlin's classic "Cheek to Cheek"? If you do, you know how Jessica felt as she tasted what would become known in Sqirl lore as "The First Toast."

That is how the cooking career of Jessica Koslow began.

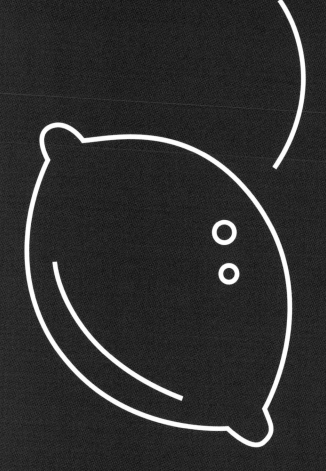

"Heaven, I'm in heaven
And my heart beats so that I can hardly speak
And I seem to find the happiness I seek
When we're out together dancing cheek to cheek"

Mirabelle Plums, Andy's Orchard

Jams
182—201

Do thoughts of making jam and other preserves evoke memories of your zaftig grandmother, Florence, canning too many pints of dilly beans? (Welcome to my world.) If you are someone who is skeptical about whether or not jam making can be cool, let me introduce you to the Zen Art of Making Sqirl Jams. I find preserving to be therapeutic and meditative—perfect for my only-child self—although having a sibling or friend with you in the kitchen will help the canning process move along much more smoothly. And I never have to worry; there's always enough to share.

COPPER POT

Owning a copper jam pan is like owning a really nice leather jacket. It makes everything around it better. It's definitely expensive, but because it's such high quality, you'll get a lot of use out of it for a long time.

The kind of pan that you cook your jam in will make a big difference in how the jam turns out. Part of that is the way the heat is conducted. Copper is an even conductor, so whatever temperature the pan is on the bottom, it'll also be that same temperature on the sides. Steel pans, on the other hand, get way hotter around the sides than on the bottom, and you end up with jam cooking unevenly and sometimes burning. So, if you're using a copper pan, you don't have to babysit the jam. But if you use steel, you'll need to keep stirring pretty much the whole time. Heavy-bottomed Dutch ovens work really well and are a good substitute for copper pans.

The pan comes first and foremost. It's really the most important tool I use.

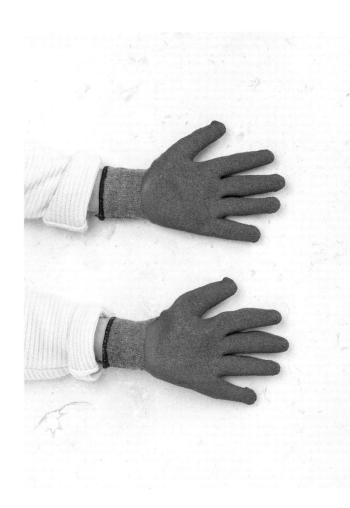

GLOVES

I wear gardening gloves when I make jam. They are rubber on one side and mesh on the other side. The cool thing about them is I can pick up hot copper pans, take baking sheets out of the oven, screw on lids, and flip over hot jars with them on. I don't need to use towels or oven mitts or anything else. It's true that jam could splatter on the mesh side and if that is something that concerns you, then you should consider wearing triple-dipped PVA gloves. They're long and they'll protect you. You can get burning hot liquid on the outside of them, and you'll never feel it.

A REALLY LONG AND HEAT-RESISTANT SPATULA

The longer the better, so that your hands aren't too close to the pot.

TURKEY STUFFING BAG

These are great because you can put spices, herbs, and lemon rinds in the bag and then tie the bag onto the handle of the jam pan. The other great thing is these bags can be washed and reused. If you don't have a turkey stuffing bag, use a double-thick piece of cheesecloth and some kitchen twine to make a little sachet.

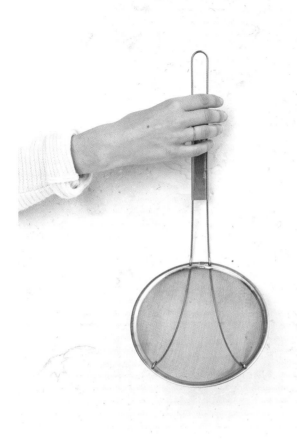

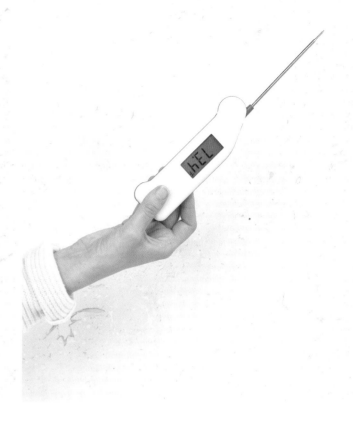

A FINE-MESH SKIMMER

You'll use this to skim off any scum that rises to the surface of the jam as it cooks. Pour some water into a bowl and set the skimmer in it. The water helps to clean the skimmer in between skimmings.

THERMAPEN

This is important for measuring the jam's temperature. I always do the plate test (see page 190) in addition to taking the temperature, and it's nice to have both methods in place to help make sure you're on the right track. I tend to put the thermometer in the pan so that the probe is resting directly on the bottom. It'll tell you the temperature of the pan, which is good information to know because if we're looking for the jam to reach 217°F (103°C) and the pan itself is less than 200°F (95°C), then why would the jam be any hotter?

SCALE

Important for precisely measuring ingredients.

A LADLE AND A HEAT-RESISTANT CONTAINER WITH A POUR SPOUT

Once the jam is done, I ladle it into the container and then it's easy to quickly fill the jars.

JARS AND LIDS

These should be washed with hot, soapy water, then left to dry. Set the clean jars upright on a rimmed baking sheet and set the lids off to the side.

DAMPENED, CLEAN PAPER TOWELS

For wiping the rims of the jars.

A FEW SMALL PLATES

Stick these in the freezer before you start cooking the jam. They'll help you decide when the jam is done. To perform something called the plate test, turn off the heat under the pot and spoon a little bit of jam onto one of the frozen plates. Put the plate back in the freezer for 1 minute, then set your pointer finger on the plate and slide it upward through the jam. If the jam parts like the Red Sea and furrows like a brow, it's done.

Canning

In terms of the actual canning process, you could follow the USDA *Complete Guide to Home Canning*. It's a very safe way to make jam at home—it involves boiling the filled jars in a big pot of water for a specified length of time, depending on the type of jam. At Sqirl, we use a different method that is more common for commercial canning. Rather than use two-part lids, we use lug lids, which are just as safe but require a different process. All the jam recipes in this chapter can be cooked, poured into jars, and then processed according to the USDA guidelines. Or the filled jars can be put straight into the refrigerator (instead of the pantry) and eaten within two weeks. If you're interested in processing lug-lid jars the way we do it, there are a few important steps to keep in mind.

First, to get your kitchen ready for making jam, put your jam pot on the stove and keep all your tools to the side. Set the jars on a baking sheet and place in a 225°F (110°C) oven for at least 20 minutes. You can leave the jars in the oven while you make the jam. The goal is to have both the jars and the jam at around the same temperature when you fill the jars.

Next, make jam! There are many different Sqirl jams to choose from. In this chapter you'll find recipes for five different jams, each a little different. I've tried to give you winning formulas for a handful of fundamental jams so that you can get started and feel confident.

Once you've cooked the jam, you need to put it in jars. While wearing gloves, pull the baking sheet out of the oven (keep the oven on) and fill each jar, leaving ¼ inch (6 mm) of headspace. Use dampened, clean paper towels to wipe the rims. Screw on the lug lids just to the point of resistance, then flip the jars over and let them rest for 2 minutes. This helps to build pressure inside the jar and force out the air. It's so much better to have two people when you're making jam because one person can ladle and the other person can pour. One person can wipe and one person can seal. It makes it safer. Flip the jars right side up and put them back into the oven, which should still be set to 225°F (110°C). Leave them in the oven to pasteurize for 25 minutes.

Let's say you're concerned that you didn't pasteurize the jam for long enough, or you're worried you were too slow to fill the jars and get the lids on. You can always take one jar out of the oven, unscrew the lid, and use the Thermapen to measure the temperature of the jam inside the jar. The magic number is 210°F (99°C). If the jam reaches 210°F (99°C), then it's safe to store in your pantry. If your Thermapen tells you that the jam is only 206°F (97°C), you can re-cover that particular jar and store it in the refrigerator, where it will keep safely for months. Then just leave the other jars in the oven for another 5 to 10 minutes to make sure they get hot enough.

Lastly, let the jars cool, then check that the lug lids have sealed. The center of the lid should be concave. If any lids failed to seal, put those jars in the refrigerator. All sealed jars are safe to keep in your pantry, away from direct sunlight.

Raspberry cardamom jam

If you're new to jam making, start here. This raspberry jam sets up pretty easily and is just delicious. Enough said.

Makes about six ½-pint (240-ml) jars (VV, GF)

¾ teaspoon whole cardamom seeds (from about 9 pods)

3 pounds 5 ounces (1.5 kg) raspberries

5 cups (1 kg) sugar

2 tablespoons fresh lemon juice (reserve the squeezed lemon)

Preheat the oven to 225°F (110°C) and get your kitchen ready for canning (see page 191).

In a small, dry pan over medium-low heat, toast the cardamom seeds—the little black things inside the green pods, not the pods themselves—for about 4 minutes, stirring every so often so they don't burn. Transfer the seeds to a cutting board and use the back of a spoon (or a mortar and pestle) to crush them to a powder, then set aside for adding later on.

You can blend the raspberries in a few different ways. Option 1: Put the berries in a large bowl and use your hands to crush them. (Choose this option if you're having a bad day.) Option 2: Put the berries in the bowl of a food processor fitted with a metal blade and process only until they are chopped but still a little bit chunky. (This is what we do.) Option 3: For a balance of textures, puree half the berries using the food processor and squeeze the other half with your hands.

Put the berries in a large bowl and stir in the sugar and lemon juice; let sit for at least a few minutes or up to 30 minutes if you have the time.

Transfer the mixture to the jam pot. Put the squeezed lemon rinds in a turkey stuffing bag and tie the bag to one of the pot's handles.

Cook over high heat, stirring and scraping the bottom of the pot so the sugars don't burn. Use a fine-mesh skimmer to skim off any white scum. There won't be a ton, but there'll be some. It's okay to turn off the heat, skim, then turn the heat back on. As the jam cooks, the solids will separate from the liquids and then rejoin. You'll see the surface will look matte at the beginning, then all of a sudden it'll change to shiny and glossy. Sometimes with raspberry jam, for whatever reason, the surface will form what look like dry patches. At this point, don your industrial gloves and use tongs to lift up the bag, squeeze out all the liquid inside, and remove the bag from the pot. Continue cooking the jam for another minute.

It's easy to tell if this jam is finished cooking because it shows very clearly on the plate test (see page 190). It usually takes 10 to 12 minutes and will be approximately 217°F (103°C) when it's done.

Remove from the heat and stir in the cardamom. Pour the jam into hot, sterilized jars, leaving ¼ inch (6 mm) of headspace. Screw on the tops just to the point of resistance, then flip the jars over and let them rest for 2 minutes. Flip them right side up and put them on a rimmed baking sheet and into the preheated oven for 25 minutes. Let cool, check the seals, and store.

Blenheim apricot and its kernel jam

Blenheims are a special variety of apricot listed on the Slow Food Ark of Taste. They were grown in California in the early 1900s, fell out of favor for a while because they don't travel well, and recently made a revival in farmers' markets, which is exactly where you should try to buy them. Eaten fresh, they're flavorful but not overwhelmingly so. Turned into jam, they are silky apricot sorcery.

Makes about six ½-pint (240-ml) jars (VV, GF)

3 pounds 5 ounces (1.5 kg) ripe Blenheim
  apricots

4½ cups (900 g) sugar
2 tablespoons fresh lemon juice

Cut the apricots in half through the north and south poles, pressing your knife along the seam that runs lengthwise. These are freestone fruits, so the pit will pop right out. Save two pits and discard the rest.

Wrap the reserved pits in a kitchen towel, crack them open using a hammer, and remove the cream-colored, soft kernels inside. Toast the kernels in a small, dry skillet over medium heat, shaking the pan every so often, for about 10 minutes.

In a large bowl, toss the apricot halves with the sugar and lemon juice. Allow the fruit to macerate for at least 30 minutes. It's even better to let it sit, covered with parchment directly touching the surface of the fruit, overnight, if you have the luxury of time. Lucky you if you do!

Preheat the oven to 225°F (110°C) and get your kitchen ready for canning.

Transfer the fruit mixture to the jam pot. Place the toasted kernels in a turkey stuffing bag and tie the bag to one of the pot's handles. Cook over high heat, stirring frequently and scraping your spatula along the bottom of the pot. If any white scum rises to the surface, turn off the heat, then quickly skim the scum and turn the heat back on. At first the mixture will look like clumps of fruit, but then as the jam cooks all the clumps will start breaking apart and blending into one another.

Once the jam looks thick and glossy and is bubbling evenly, use tongs to lift up the bag and squeeze out all the liquid inside. Discard the bag and the kernels inside it. Let the jam cook for another minute, then use an instant-read thermometer to measure the temperature. At around 215°F (102°C), remove from the heat and do a plate test (see page 190) to check for doneness. The exact cooking time will depend on the pot you are using, but it usually takes somewhere around 10 to 20 minutes.

Pour the jam into hot, sterilized jars, leaving ¼ inch (6 mm) of headspace. Screw on the tops just to the point of resistance, then flip the jars over and let them rest for 2 minutes. Flip them right side up and put them on a rimmed baking sheet and into the preheated oven for 25 minutes. Let cool, check the seals, and store.

NOTE ON RIPE FRUIT

Make sure to use ripe, soft fruit. If you use a rock-hard apricot, straight off the supermarket shelf, it will not break down and you'll end up with chunky, hard bits of fruit surrounded by a semiformed jam/syrup situation—not one's finest hour. So, if you buy firm fruit, eat some fresh and let the rest sit out for a few days until they have softened.

PUBLIC SERVICE ANNOUNCEMENT

Do not eat the raw apricot kernels.

Strawberry rose geranium jam

Get ready. Strawberry jam without the addition of pectin is a very challenging jam to make. This fruit is full of water and you're going to need to remove that water in order to create jam. As it gets closer and closer to being done, this jam bubbles like angry lava.

Makes about six ½-pint (240-ml) jars (VV, GF)

3 pounds 5 ounces (1.5 kg) stemmed
  strawberries
4½ cups plus 2 tablespoons (920 g) sugar

2 tablespoons fresh lemon juice (reserve the
  squeezed lemon)
A few sprigs (7 g) of fresh rose geranium **(see Notes)**

Cut the strawberries in half and puree them using a food processor or an immersion blender. Pour the strawberries into a large bowl and stir in the sugar and lemon juice. (Don't throw out the lemon rinds.) Let the fruit macerate, covered with parchment directly touching the surface of the fruit, for at least 30 minutes. If you can let it sit overnight, the fruit will absorb more sugar and take a lot less time to cook. Also, it'll be a lot less violent when it bubbles.

Preheat the oven to 225°F (110°C) and get your kitchen ready for canning (see page 191).

Transfer the strawberry mixture to the jam pot. Put the lemon rinds in a turkey stuffing bag along with the rose geranium, and tie the bag to one of the pot's handles.

Cook over high heat, continuously stirring and scraping the bottom of the pot so that the sugars don't burn. Pretty quickly a large amount of white scum will form on the surface. Turn off the heat, use a spatula on the surface of the jam to round up all the scum, skim the scum, then turn the heat back on. Then say "Skim the scum" three times fast.

Repeat the cooking and skimming process, turning off the heat only as needed. If you can skim without turning off the heat, that will be best because your goal is to cook the jam in the shortest amount of time possible so that there's very little caramelization of the sugars. You're never going to be able to get all the scum. At some point, it just starts pulling back into the jam. Make sure you protect yourself with gloves. Sometimes it feels like you need a full-body shield.

After you've skimmed the scum and the jam is clear and bubbling, use tongs to lift up the bag and squeeze out all the liquid inside. You really want to squeeze all the pectin from the lemon rinds into the pot because strawberries have such a small amount of natural pectin. Remove the bag, discarding the rinds and rose geranium inside it.

Continue cooking until the jam starts looking thick and glossy, 10 to 15 minutes. To check for doneness, it is tricky to get close enough to measure the temperature of this jam (because of all that violent bubbling). A better strategy is to use the plate test (see page 190).

Pour the jam into hot, sterilized jars, leaving ¼ inch (6 mm) of headspace. Screw on the tops just to the point of resistance, then flip the jars over and let them rest for 2 minutes. Flip them right side up and put them on a rimmed baking sheet and into the preheated oven for 25 minutes. Let cool, check the seals, and store.

NOTE ON STRAWBERRY JAM

Strawberries have very little pectin and a lot of water, so this jam will not be a super-thick, pectin-rich jam. But it will taste like ripe strawberries in a rose garden, so the consolation prize is a good one.

CAN'T FIND ROSE GERANIUM?

You can make this jam with lemon verbena or some other herb, or you can just make it without any herb. Think of this recipe as the vanilla ice cream of strawberry jam recipes; it's a good base to which you can add your favorite flavors.

Shady Lady tomato and coriander jam

Shady Lady tomatoes have more going for them than just a great name.
They are a farmers' market favorite, an all-purpose tomato with good flavor. We turn
them into savory jam, which is sort of like our version of ketchup, only a bit spicier.
Schmearing a little on a grilled cheese sandwich is my go-to move.

Makes about four ½-pint (240-ml) jars (VV, GF)

2 scant tablespoons coriander seeds
3 pounds 5 ounces (1.5 kg) ripe red Shady Lady
tomatoes **(see Note)**

2¼ cups (450 g) sugar
2 teaspoons fine sea salt

In a small, dry skillet over medium-low heat, toast the coriander seeds until they are fragrant, about 4 minutes. Remove from the heat and use the back of a spoon or a mortar and pestle to grind about one-third of the seeds to a powder. Set both the whole coriander and the ground coriander aside for adding later on.

Cut the tomatoes in half and cut out their cores. Using an immersion blender or a food processor, puree the tomatoes until they're saucy. Put the tomatoes in a large bowl, then stir in the sugar and salt. They don't have to macerate for long, but there should be some sort of marriage between the fruit and the sugar. If you do have the time, it'll only help to let them sit, covered with parchment paper directly touching the surface of the fruit, overnight at room temperature.

Transfer the tomato mixture to the jam pot. Cook over high heat, stirring often, until you see white scum form on the surface. Skim it off, then keep cooking and skimming until most of the scum is skimmed. It'll form forever, but there's a point at which the scum falls back onto itself. At that point, stop skimming and add both the whole and ground coriander.

Continue to cook the tomato jam until it has reduced in volume by around half or a bit more. It usually takes a good hour and change. To know when it is done, I look for rings around the pot that tell me how much

jam there was and now is, like the rings of a tree trunk. There should be one ring for how high the tomato jam was when it started cooking, and then you can estimate where one-half that amount would be. The finished tomato jam will be a little loose and glossy, although it's important to know that it never hits that thick, super-glossy jam texture.

When the tomato jam is almost done, preheat the oven to 225°F (110°C) and get your kitchen ready for canning (see page 191).

Pour the jam into hot, sterilized jars, leaving ¼ inch (6 mm) of headspace. Screw on the tops just to the point of resistance, then flip the jars over and let them rest for 2 minutes. Flip them right side up and put them on a rimmed baking sheet and into the preheated oven for 25 minutes. Let cool, check the seals, and store.

NOTE ON TOMATOES

We use a variety of tomato called Shady Lady that we buy from Debbie Wong of Wong Farms. I love her tomatoes. We make this jam only when it's the peak of the season, and we always make it with tomato seconds. Go to your farmers' market and ask a tomato farmer for seconds, which are usually half the price of the perfect-looking tomatoes. Make sure they're red, because if they are yellow and green, your jam will turn out brown.

Spiced Gravenstein apple butter

Walker Apples (in Sebastopol, California) is the place to be.

Makes about three ½-pint (240-ml) jars (VV, GF)

4 pounds (1.8 kg) Gravenstein apples **(see Notes)**
2 bay leaves
½ teaspoon whole cloves
1 cinnamon stick

½ teaspoon whole black peppercorns
2¼ cups (540 g) sugar
1 tablespoon fresh lemon juice
¼ teaspoon freshly grated nutmeg

Cut the apples into quarters, leaving the stem, peel, and core where they are. Poach in a large pot of boiling water until the fruit is soft all the way through but not falling apart, about 15 minutes.

Meanwhile, combine the bay leaves, cloves, cinnamon stick, and peppercorns in a dry skillet set over medium-low heat. Toast, moving the pan every so often, until the smell reminds you of the holidays, about 3 minutes.

Drain the apples, then run them through a food mill. Weigh the milled pulp—there should be about 2 pounds (910 g). If you have more or less apple pulp, you can figure out how much sugar and lemon juice you'll need to add by doing the following calculations:

grams of milled apple pulp x 0.6 =
grams of sugar

grams of milled apple pulp x 0.0175 =
grams of lemon juice

While the pulp is warm, stir in the sugar and lemon juice, then transfer the mixture to the jam pot. Put the toasted spices in a turkey stuffing bag and tie the bag to one of the pot's handles.

Cook over low heat for 2 to 3 hours. You don't need to stir that often in the beginning; the apple butter can just do its thing. I find myself checking in on it periodically while making dinner and watching *Seinfeld* reruns. You'll notice that over the course of several hours, the liquid in the pot will separate from the solids, and then, just before the apple butter is done, they will reunite. Close to the end, it will form a skin and bubble like crazy. At this point, don your industrial gloves and use tongs to lift up the bag of spices and squeeze out all the liquid inside. (There's a good amount of liquid that will come out.) Remove the bag, discarding the spices inside it. Stir and continue cooking for a minute or so, then check for doneness by performing the plate test (see page 190). It's easy to overcook this jam and overcaramelize the sugars, so make sure to carefully check for doneness— it should be just a touch thicker than applesauce. Err on the side of under doing it because saucy apple butter is better than rock-hard apple butter. Ask anyone.

When the apple butter is almost done, preheat the oven to 225°F (110°C) and get your kitchen ready for canning (see page 191).

Remove the apple butter from the heat and stir in the nutmeg. Moving quickly so that it stays super hot, pour it into hot, sterilized jars, leaving ¼ inch (6 mm) of headspace. Screw on the tops just to the point of resistance, then flip the jars over and let them rest for 2 minutes. Flip them right side up and put them on a rimmed baking sheet and into the preheated oven for 30 minutes. Let cool, check the seals, and store.

NOTE ON GRAVENSTEINS

All apples are not created equal. This variety really is unique. It's floral; it has good acidity. It develops a blush color as it cooks. That rough toothiness you sometimes find in other apple butters? You don't get it with this. There is no true substitution. Here's the one time I will say, "Substitutions politely declined."

Okay, okay, you can make this with a different apple; choose a tart one. But then you definitely have to come to Sqirl and try Gravenstein apple butter. You know, as a taste test.

NOTE ON CANNING APPLE BUTTERS

You want to fill the jars while the apple butter is hot hot hot. If the apple butter cools off, it (1) starts to congeal really quickly and (2) will form bubbles throughout the jar, which is bad because it's an opportunity for oxygen to reach the apple butter.

NO FOOD MILL?

That's okay. Your apple butter won't be quite as smooth, but you can peel and core the apples before boiling them, then puree to a pulp using a food processor or blender. Be especially careful not to boil the peeled apples too long—they will fall apart more easily without the skins on.

C is for Cookie. It's good enough for Susan Power

Desserts
202—237

A pastry at breakfast or with an afternoon coffee just makes sense, so we end up serving a lot of pastries at Sqirl. Our pastry chef, Meadow Ramsey, has been with me since the beginning. She has this unbelievable ability to create really smart baked goods for a huge swath of people. We get customers asking for gluten-free cakes, vegan pastries, nut-free cookies, you name it. And Meadow comes up with these baked goods that at first glance seem like things you've encountered before. They're disarmingly friendly. But once you take a bite, you realize that this isn't the same old chocolate chip cookie you thought you knew. This one is way more chocolatey, and you start to wonder why all the chocolate chip cookies you've eaten in your life weren't as good. That vaguely banana-bread-looking slice of loaf cake over there? Oh, it's vegan and made from carrots. You may look into the Sqirl pastry case and spot a familiar muffin. Try a piece of it and you'll be surprised to encounter the taste and texture of a doughnut. Meadow plays with flavor and toys with expectation, all while accommodating the many different desires of our customers.

Flaky-ass biscuits

Living in Atlanta, I spent a majority of my caloric intake on biscuits. Now, with these biscuits on the menu every Sunday at Sqirl, I guess I'm attempting to relive those years. The goal: to make them as flaky as possible without using self-rising flour or lard (so as to keep them vegetarian).

Serve these warm, with good jam (see pages 182–201) and butter on the side, if you desire.

Makes about 18 (2-inch/5-cm) biscuits (V)

4 cups (500 g) all-purpose flour, plus more for rolling
2 tablespoons sugar
1¾ teaspoons baking powder
¾ teaspoon baking soda
2 teaspoons fine sea salt

1 cup plus 2 tablespoons (1¼ sticks/250 g) very cold unsalted butter, diced; plus 4 tablespoons (½ stick/60 g) at room temperature
1¼ cups (300 ml) buttermilk, plus more for brushing
Fleur de sel

In the bowl of a stand mixer fitted with the paddle attachment, combine the flour, sugar, baking powder, baking soda, salt, and the cold butter pieces. Mix on low speed to break up and distribute the butter. After 30 seconds or so, while the mixer is still mixing, slowly pour in the buttermilk. Once the dough comes together, stop the machine and scrape down the sides and across the bottom of the bowl. If you uncover a stash of flour stuck to the bottom of the bowl, mix for another few seconds. Turn the dough out onto a floured surface, then quickly but gently shape it into a 10 by 7–inch (25 by 17–cm) rectangle about 1 inch (2.5 cm) thick.

Position the dough so that the long sides of the rectangle are parallel to your shoulders. Imagine dividing the dough vertically into thirds. Spread the softened butter evenly across the left two-thirds of the dough, leaving the right third naked. Use your right hand to fold the naked third over the middle third, then use your left hand to fold the left third on top of that, stacking it to create three layers of dough. (It's okay if it cracks where it folds.) Wrap with plastic and refrigerate for 30 minutes.

Remove the dough from the fridge and position it so that the long sides of the rectangle are, once again, parallel to your shoulders. Roll it out to a 15 by 9–inch (38 by 23–cm) rectangle about ¾ inch (2 cm) thick, sprinkling with flour as needed to prevent sticking. Fold into a stack just as you did before, this time without any butter. Wrap with plastic and refrigerate for 30 minutes.

Repeat the rolling (to ¾ inch/2 cm thick) and folding process one more time, then refrigerate for 1 hour.

About 20 minutes before you're ready to cut and bake the biscuits, preheat the oven to 400°F (205°C). Line a baking sheet with parchment paper.

Roll out the dough to about 1 inch (2.5 cm) thick. Use a biscuit cutter or the rim of a sturdy glass to punch out 2-inch (5-cm) round biscuits. You can definitely mash the scraps together and cut the dough a second time—just know that those biscuits won't be as tender or beautiful as the first round. (These can officially be your "side pieces.")

Place the biscuits on the baking sheet, spacing them at least 1 inch (2.5 cm) apart. Brush the tops with buttermilk and sprinkle with fleur de sel. Bake until flaky and golden brown, about 25 minutes.

Transfer the biscuits to a wire rack and let cool for a few minutes. These are best eaten right away.

Hazelnut financiers

Hazelnut financiers
choose your fruit

Meadow says you can use any kind of nut for these, but she also says the robust flavor of hazelnuts complements the deep, dark flavor of buckwheat flour. That's why she's the boss.

Makes 12 (2 by 4–inch/5 by 10–cm) financiers (V, GF)

¾ cup (100 g) hazelnuts
⅓ cup (50 g) buckwheat flour **(see Note)**
1¼ cups (150 g) confectioners' sugar, sifted
½ teaspoon fine sea salt
½ cup (1 stick/115 g) unsalted butter, plus more
   for the pans

4 large egg whites
Fresh fruit, such as 6 kumquats, sliced and
   seeded; 12 small strawberries, hulled and
   quartered lengthwise; 1 peach, pitted and sliced
   into thin wedges; or ½ apple, cored and sliced
Granulated sugar

Preheat the oven to 350°F (175°C). Place the hazelnuts on a rimmed baking sheet and toast them in the oven, stirring once or twice, for 8 to 10 minutes.

Let cool slightly, then wrap the toasted hazelnuts in a kitchen towel and rub off as much of their papery skins as you can and let cool completely. Once the nuts are completely cool, grind them to a fine meal using a food processor, then transfer to a large bowl. Whisk in the buckwheat flour, confectioners' sugar, and salt.

Place the butter in a heavy pan over medium heat. Cook until the butter has melted and the milk solids have browned on the bottom of the pan, about 10 minutes, then remove from the heat and let cool for a few minutes.

Whisk the egg whites until they're foamy, then whisk them into the hazelnut mixture. Gradually whisk in the browned butter. Cover and chill the batter in the refrigerator for at least 2 hours. (An overnight rest is great.)

When you're ready to bake the financiers, preheat the oven to 375°F (190°C) and liberally butter 12 (2 by 4–inch/5 by 10–cm) financier tins. Really, butter them as liberally as your bubbe would if she were making these for you on your birthday. Scoop a rounded spoonful of batter into each well, filling it no more than halfway. Top each with a slice or two of fruit, then sprinkle lightly with granulated sugar. Bake until the edges are golden brown, 20 to 25 minutes, depending on the size and type of tin. Let cool in the tins for several minutes, then turn out onto a wire rack.

These are best eaten the day they are made.

YOU DON'T HAVE FANCY FINANCIER TINS?
Use mini-muffin tins, regular muffin tins, 3½-inch (9-cm) round tart pans, or any little baking molds you have. Remember to liberally butter the tins. The baking time will change a bit depending on the size of the mold, so look for the edges to become golden brown and for the center to puff.

NOTE ON BUCKWHEAT FLOUR
At Sqirl we use white buckwheat flour, which imparts a light color to the financiers. If you choose to use darker buckwheat flour, the financiers will have a deeper color and a slightly stronger, earthy, mineral flavor. Give it a whirl and find out which type of flour you like best.

Valrhona fleur de sel chocolate cookies

Valrhona fleur de sel chocolate cookies

To know me is to know that I add fleur de sel to finish just about everything.

Makes about 18 cookies (V)

2 cups (250 g) all-purpose flour
⅔ cup (55 g) unsweetened cocoa powder
    (the darker the better)
1½ teaspoons baking soda
Pinch of fine sea salt
1 cup (2 sticks/225 g) unsalted butter, at room
    temperature

¾ cup (165 g) packed brown sugar
⅓ cup plus 1 tablespoon (80 g) granulated sugar
1 teaspoon vanilla extract
9 ounces (250 g) 70 to 85% cacao Valrhona
    chocolate **(see Note)**, chopped into chips
Fleur de sel

In a bowl, stir together the flour, cocoa powder, baking soda, and salt.

In another bowl, using electric beaters or a stand mixer fitted with the paddle attachment, cream the butter, brown sugar, granulated sugar, and vanilla until exceptionally fluffy, about 7 minutes. Slowly add the flour mixture, then stir in the chopped chocolate. (The dough is pretty stiff; don't be surprised by that.)

Wrap the cookie dough in plastic and chill it in the refrigerator for at least a few hours. (We usually make the dough in the late afternoon and let it chill overnight. There's nothing wrong with letting it chill for several days.)

Preheat the oven to 350°F (175°C). Line two baking sheets with parchment paper.

Shape the cookie dough into 1¼-ounce (35-g) balls (a little larger than Ping-Pong balls) and place them, spaced a couple of inches apart, on the prepared baking sheets. Sprinkle each with a pinch of fleur de sel.

Bake for 5 minutes, switch the position of the baking sheets in the oven, and then bake for 6 minutes more. When they come out of the oven, they should have a dark, sexy sheen to them. While they're still hot, we use a round cookie cutter to make the edges of the cookies perfectly round, but that step is definitely not necessary. However, you should know that the little scraps that result are possibly the best snack in this book. Let cool on the baking sheets.

These are best when just barely cool enough that they can be picked up, still gooey and fresh. However, they will keep, covered, at room temperature for a few days. You can refresh them by warming them in a 325°F (160°C) oven for 4 to 5 minutes.

NOTE ON CHOCOLATE
If you can't find Valrhona chocolate (Trader Joe's sells it!), you can use any super-good 70 to 85% cacao chocolate. I first encountered Valrhona chocolate when I worked at Bacchanalia, at the beginning of my career in the kitchen, so it fills me with a certain nostalgia for those days. At Sqirl we make ganache with Guittard, which is another high-quality chocolate you can try.

Coconut rice pudding with lemon curd and coconut croutons

Coconut rice pudding with lemon curd and coconut croutons

I recognize that there's a things-in-bowls trend happening right now. We have so many jam jars at the restaurant that we have a things-in-jars situation going on. If you have extra fresh fruit in the house, try layering it into this, using any kind of bowl or jar you like.

Serves 6 (VV, GFO)

FOR THE LEMON CURD

3 lemons with nice, smooth, oily skin
½ cup (50 g) sugar
1½ cups (360 ml) non-GMO canola oil or other neutral-flavored oil

FOR THE COCONUT CROUTONS

3 slices white bread or ¼ baguette (about 100 g total)
1½ tablespoons coconut oil, melted
1½ tablespoons sugar

FOR THE COCONUT RICE PUDDING

4 cups (960 ml) unsweetened or very lightly sweetened almond milk (page 264 or store-bought)
1 (13-ounce/400-ml) can unsweetened coconut milk
½ cup (100 g) sugar
Pinch of fine sea salt
1 vanilla bean
6 cardamom pods
1½ cups (300 g) medium-grain brown rice

MAKE THE LEMON CURD

Use a vegetable peeler to remove the zest from the lemons. Try not to press too hard; ideally, you'll remove just the peel and almost none of the bitter white pith. A Y-shaped peeler works best. If there's a lot of pith clinging to the underside of the zest pieces, you can go back and use a sharp knife to trim it off, but it's a pain. Much better to do it right the first time around.

Squeeze the peeled lemons and reserve all the juice.

Place the zest pieces in a small pot, cover with water, and bring to a boil. When the water boils, drain the zest in a colander. Return the zest pieces to the pot, cover with water, and bring to a boil again. Drain, then repeat the process one more time.

Return the zest pieces to the pot and add the sugar and the lemon juice. Bring to a simmer, then reduce the heat to low, cover the pot with a tight-fitting lid, and cook for 30 minutes. Let cool slightly.

While the lemon mixture is still hot, transfer it to a high-speed blender and blend until nearly smooth, starting on the lowest setting and gradually increasing the speed to high. Stop the machine and scrape down the sides. Turn it back on low speed and slowly—very, very slowly— pour in the oil while you gradually increase the speed. The mixture will be thick and smooth. Don't worry if there are little flecks of lemon zest. Transfer the curd to a heat-safe container, cover the surface directly with a piece of plastic wrap, and refrigerate until cold, about 2 hours. It'll thicken a little more as it cools. (The lemon curd will keep in the refrigerator for about 1 week. If it separates, just whisk vigorously and it should come back together.)

MAKE THE COCONUT CROUTONS

Preheat the oven to 350°F (180°C). Slice away the crust of the bread, then cut the bread into tiny (no bigger than ½-inch/12-mm square) croutons. Put the croutons in a bowl, add the coconut oil and sugar, and toss to coat, squeezing the bread gently so it absorbs the oil. Spread the croutons out on a rimmed baking sheet. Bake, stirring and flipping the croutons once or twice, until golden brown, about 12 minutes. (Coconut croutons can be made up to a week ahead and stored in an airtight container.)

MAKE THE COCONUT RICE PUDDING

In a heavy-bottomed pot, combine 2 cups (480 ml) water, the almond milk, coconut milk, sugar, and salt. Slice the vanilla bean in half lengthwise and use the back of your knife to scrape all the tiny seeds into the pot. Add the scraped bean pod to the pot as well. Crush the cardamom pods (with a pestle or the back of a knife), wrap them up in a cheesecloth sachet, and drop into the pot. (Or forget the sachet and choose to fish them out at the end.)

Bring to a simmer, stirring to dissolve the sugar. Add the rice. Cook at a very gentle simmer, stirring as needed to prevent sticking and burning, until the rice is tender and the liquid has reduced in volume such that the rice is no longer fully submerged, about 1 hour.

Pour the pudding into a shallow dish. Remove and discard the cardamom sachet and vanilla bean pod. Place a piece of plastic wrap directly against the surface of the pudding, place in the refrigerator, and let cool completely. (If, after cooling for a while, the pudding seems too thick for your liking, you can thin it with a splash of almond milk or coconut milk.)

To serve, spoon some of the rice pudding into little bowls. Top each with a dollop of lemon curd and a small handful of coconut croutons.

WANT TO FREEZE THIS PUDDING LIKE NACHO ALEGRE DID?

Spoon it into ice cube molds and chill in the freezer until solid. Nacho is just a big kid having fun with food. I recommend you also freeze some ice cubes of pomegranate arils or thinly sliced kumquats (as shown in the photo on page 210) because then you can add them to drinks.

GLUTEN-FREE OPTION

Leave off the coconut croutons.

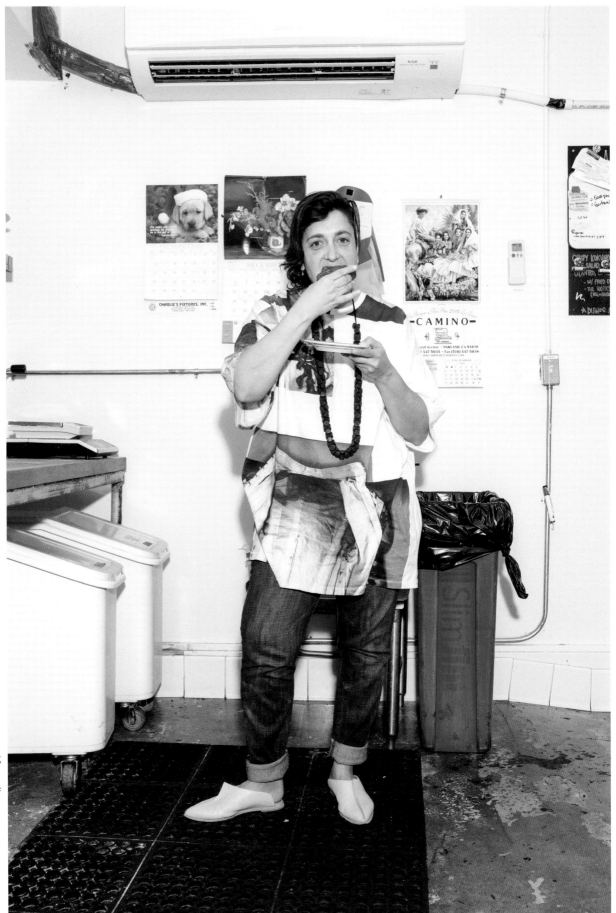

Inbal Waldman works the (pastry) room

Carrot-ginger black sesame loaf

Carrot-ginger black sesame loaf

The more sesame seeds you can put on top of this loaf, the better. It can get crumbly, but it's good for you because you get to eat all the crumbs. Also, I'd be playing tricks on you if I didn't tell you that this treat is the perfect color combination for Halloween.

Makes 1 (8½ by 4½–inch/21.5 by 11–cm) loaf (VV)

½ cup (120 ml) vegetable oil, plus more for the pan
2 cups (250 g) all-purpose flour, plus more for
   the pan
1½ teaspoons baking powder
2 teaspoons ground cinnamon
⅔ cup (135 g) granulated sugar
⅔ cup (145 g) packed brown sugar
½ cup (120 ml) unsweetened applesauce
⅓ cup (80 ml) almond milk (page 264 or
   store-bought)
2-inch (5-cm) piece of ginger, peeled and
   finely grated
1 teaspoon vanilla extract
¾ teaspoon fine sea salt
2 large carrots (7 ounces/200 g total),
   coarsely grated
2 to 3 tablespoons black sesame seeds

Preheat the oven to 350°F (175°C). Brush the inside surfaces of an 8½ by 4½–inch (21.5 by 11–cm) loaf pan with a little oil. Dust with flour, tapping out any excess.

In a small bowl, combine the flour, baking powder, and cinnamon.

In a large bowl, whisk together the granulated sugar, brown sugar, applesauce, almond milk, ginger, vanilla, and salt. Using a rubber spatula, fold in the flour mixture, followed by the carrots, and finally the oil.

Scrape the batter into the prepared pan and sprinkle the top with the sesame seeds. You want it to be completely covered in seeds. Bake until the middle of the loaf has puffed and a toothpick inserted into the center comes out clean, about 1 hour 10 minutes.

Let cool completely in the pan before slicing.

Store, tightly wrapped, at room temperature for up to 3 days.

Powerballs

Think of these powerballs as raw, vegan, gluten-free truffles. Oh, that doesn't sound good? They are. If I were going on a hike and it was one hundred degrees outside, I'd want two of these and a huge bottle of water.

When we came up with this recipe, I had a vision of one of my employees dressed in a full-body galaxy-print spandex unitard, with a powerball in each hand, ready to shoot out her energy into the world.

Makes 20 (1½-inch/4-cm) powerballs (VV, GF)

1 tablespoon flaxseed meal **(see Note)**
2 cups (225 g) pecans (halves or pieces)
½ cup plus 1 tablespoon (130 g) packed brown
    sugar
1 teaspoon fine sea salt
1⅔ cups (145 g) unsweetened coconut flakes
4½ ounces (130 g) 70% cacao chocolate, finely
    chopped
12 pitted dates (7 ounces/200 g total)

Preheat the oven to 350°F (175°C). Line a rimmed baking sheet with parchment paper.

Put the flaxseed meal in a small bowl and use a fork to stir in 2 tablespoons warm water.

In the bowl of a food processor fitted with a metal blade, blend the pecans, brown sugar, salt, and 1⅓ cups (115 g) of the coconut until everything is finely chopped. Add the chocolate and dates and pulse until incorporated. Stop the machine and scrape down the sides of the bowl. Spoon in the flaxseed mixture—it will be gloppy. Continue blending until the batter is a little tacky, about 30 seconds more.

Spread the remaining ⅓ cup (30 g) coconut on a plate. Scoop up 1½-inch (4-cm) balls of batter, roll them between your hands, then roll in the coconut and place on the baking sheet. The coconut won't stick super well; it's okay, just do your best to press a few flakes onto each ball.

Bake until the coconut flakes are golden brown, 10 to 12 minutes.

Store, covered, at room temperature for up to 3 days.

NOTE ON FLAXSEED MEAL
Pre-ground flaxseed meal has such a short life span; it starts to go rancid after about 2 weeks. It might be easier to start with raw, whole flaxseed, which can be stored in the fridge or freezer for up to a year. To turn flaxseed into flaxseed meal, all you need to do is blitz it for about 20 seconds in a high-speed blender or a spice grinder.

RAW OPTION
You don't have to bake these. You can just roll them in any kind of chopped nuts you like, then refrigerate them to firm them up a bit. They will keep in the refrigerator for up to 1 week.

Malva pudding cakes

Just make these. You won't be sorry. Everyone will thank you and they'll wonder where you got this recipe, and you can tell them—right here, in this book!

Makes 8 cakes (V)

FOR THE CAKES

1 cup (125 g) all-purpose flour
1½ teaspoons baking powder
¾ teaspoon baking soda
1 cup plus 2 tablespoons (225 g) sugar, plus more for sprinkling
2 large eggs
¾ teaspoon fine sea salt
¼ cup (50 g) Blenheim Apricot and Its Kernel Jam (page 194 or store-bought)

1½ tablespoons unsalted butter, melted
½ teaspoon apple cider vinegar
1 cup (240 ml) whole milk

FOR THE CUSTARD FILLING

¾ cup (180 ml) heavy cream
¾ cup (150 g) sugar
½ cup (1 stick/115 g) unsalted butter

MAKE THE CAKES

Preheat the oven to 375°F (190°C). Set eight ungreased, straight-sided paper baking molds with a diameter of 2⅝ inches (6.5 cm) on a rimmed baking sheet.

In a small bowl, stir together the flour, baking powder, and baking soda. In the bowl of a stand mixer fitted with the paddle attachment, combine the sugar, eggs, and salt. Beat on medium speed until light in color but as dense and thick as pancake batter, about 2 minutes. Reduce the mixing speed to low and add the jam, butter, and vinegar, in that order. Now you're going to alternate adding the milk and the flour mixture, starting with about one-third of the milk, then about half the flour mixture, followed by another one-third of the milk, the remaining flour mixture, and finally the remaining milk.

Divide the batter among the paper molds, filling each about two-thirds full. Generously sprinkle the tops with sugar. Bake for 35 to 40 minutes, until dark golden brown. They have to be really baked—actually, almost overbaked—in order to soak up the filling, so don't pull them out of the oven until they are dark golden brown.

MAKE THE CUSTARD FILLING

In a pot, combine the cream, sugar, butter, and ¼ cup (60 ml) water. Bring to a simmer over medium heat, whisking until smooth, then remove from the heat and keep warm.

As soon as the cakes come out of the oven, use the tip of a steak knife to poke the middle of one, gently pull back the cake to open up a tiny hole, then pour in custard filling until the cake won't accept any

more. Move on to the next cake and fill it with custard. Once you've filled them all, go back and repeat the filling process a second time with any remaining custard. There's going to be overflow and that overflow is going to be delicious. We call it the Malva feet. Serve warm.

My hope is that you'd eat these right away because they're just so custardy on the inside when warm. If you don't eat them the day they are made, wrap each one in plastic and store at room temperature. The following day, unwrap and warm in a 325°F (160°C) oven for about 5 minutes.

NOTE ON PAPER MOLDS
Look for these at a kitchen supply store or order them online. They are sometimes called mini panettone molds.

Hazelnut torte with raspberry jam, ganache, and toasted meringue

Hazelnut torte with raspberry jam, ganache, and toasted meringue

When I opened Sqirl, this torte was on the menu. At first I served a slice of it with a smidge of crème fraîche on top and a dollop of jam to the side. As we've grown, so too has this torte. It's now something more like the leaning tower of torte, with layers of various fillings. If you don't feel like making the whole thing, you can make just the cake base and serve it however you like.

Makes 1 (9-inch/23-cm) torte; serves 12 (V, GF)

FOR THE HAZELNUT TORTE

Unsalted butter, for the pan
2¾ cups (370 g) hazelnuts
10 large eggs
1½ cups (300 g) sugar
½ teaspoon vanilla extract
½ teaspoon fine sea salt
½ cup (65 g) cocoa nibs

FOR THE MERINGUE

½ cup (120 ml) egg whites (from about 4 large eggs)
1 cup (200 g) sugar
1 teaspoon vanilla extract

FOR THE GANACHE AND FILLING

¾ cup (180 ml) heavy cream
6.3 ounces (180 g) 70% cacao chocolate, chopped
1 cup Raspberry Cardamom Jam (page 192 or store-bought)

MAKE THE HAZELNUT TORTE

Preheat the oven to 325°F (165°C). Butter two 9-inch (23-cm) round cake pans and line the bottoms with parchment paper. (If you'd prefer to bake the torte in a single pan, use a 10-inch/25-cm springform pan with 3-inch/7.5-cm sides. Once the cake has baked and cooled completely, use a long serrated knife to split it into two even layers.)

Spread the hazelnuts on a rimmed baking sheet. Toast in the oven, stirring once or twice, for 10 to 12 minutes. Let cool. Leave the oven on.

Separate the eggs, collecting the whites in the bowl of a stand mixer fitted with the whisk attachment and dropping the yolks into another large bowl. Whip the egg whites until they are foamy, then, while the mixer is running, gradually add ½ cup (100 g) of the sugar. Continue whipping, now on medium-high speed, to soft peaks. Beat in the vanilla.

In the bowl of a food processor fitted with a metal blade, grind the toasted hazelnuts with the remaining 1 cup (200 g) sugar and the salt. Transfer to the bowl with the egg yolks, add the cocoa nibs, and stir

very well. Fold about one-third of the beaten egg whites into the nut mixture, then fold in the remaining whites, trying to keep the batter as airy as possible.

Divide the batter evenly between the two prepared pans. Bake until the tops spring back lightly and don't jiggle when you press on them, 20 to 30 minutes. (If you bake the torte in a single 10-inch/25-cm springform pan, bake for about 1 hour. If the top is getting too brown before the cake is done, tent it with aluminum foil.)

WHILE THE CAKES BAKE, MAKE THE MERINGUE

Set up a double boiler or improvise with a heat-resistant bowl that hovers inside a pot filled with about 1 inch (2.5 cm) of water. Combine the egg whites and sugar in the bowl, whisking continuously until the sugar has dissolved completely. Remove the bowl from the heat. Using electric beaters, whisk on high speed until the meringue has cooled and formed fluffy, pillowy peaks. Mix in the vanilla.

MAKE THE GANACHE

Pour the cream into a small pot, and slowly heat it up to just under a simmer. Put the chocolate in a heat-resistant bowl, then pour the scalded cream over the chocolate and set aside for a few minutes.

Starting from the center of the bowl and working your way out to the edges, whisk quickly but gently to unite the chocolate and cream. Let cool to room temperature, whisking occasionally, about 30 minutes. (It'll thicken as it cools—you could pop it in the fridge to speed things along.)

Let the cakes cool completely in the pans, then unmold onto a wire rack and peel off the parchment. (The cakes can be made 1 day ahead and stored, loosely wrapped in plastic, at room temperature or in the refrigerator. They're not picky. They also freeze well.)

ASSEMBLE THE TORTE

Set the bottom cake layer on a serving plate. Spread the jam across it, then dollop the ganache over the jam and gently smooth it out. Place the second cake layer on top. Spread the meringue over the cake,

using a spatula or the back of a spoon to create lots of swirls, peaks, and dips. Use a kitchen torch to toast the meringue. (Alternatively, you can toast the meringue under the broiler—watch it like a hawk so it doesn't burn.)

Slice and serve right away. If, for some strange reason, there are slices of cake left over, place a tall glass or bottle next to the cake and loosely tent with plastic. The bottle helps prevent the plastic from sticking directly on top of the already rather sticky toasted meringue.

NOTE ON GANACHE

Do you have any extra ganache left over from the Grown-up Kid, Part 1 (page 39)? You can use it here! Or you can use this one there. That other one is a sweeter ganache, and I prefer a slightly darker ganache to accompany this torte. Just saying: Use it, don't lose it.

David Giambruno, check(ed)

Upside-down cake
season dictates pear, plum, or blood orange

Please don't run to the store just to buy one orange. If you have all the other ingredients for this cake but not the orange zest, just add ground cinnamon or cardamom instead.

Makes 1 (10-inch/25-cm) cake; serves 12 (V)

FOR THE CARAMEL "TOPPING"

½ cup (1 stick/115 g) unsalted butter, plus more for the pan
½ cup (110 g) packed brown sugar
Pinch of fine sea salt

FOR THE CAKE

2 cups (250 g) all-purpose flour
1½ teaspoons baking powder
½ teaspoon baking soda

1 cup (2 sticks/225 g) unsalted butter, at room temperature
1 cup (200 g) granulated sugar
Grated zest of 1 orange
2 teaspoons vanilla extract
¾ teaspoon fine sea salt
3 large eggs
¾ cup (180 ml) buttermilk
4 or 5 small plums (1 pound/455 g total), pitted and sliced; if plums are not in season use either pears or blood oranges (see Notes)

Preheat the oven to 350°F (180°C). Butter a 10-inch (25-cm) round cake pan with 3-inch (7.5-cm) sides, then line the bottom with parchment paper and butter the parchment as well.

MAKE THE CARAMEL "TOPPING"

In a small pot set over low heat, stir together the butter, brown sugar, and salt. Once the butter has melted, whisk it to combine completely with the sugar, then pour it into the prepared pan and spread it out evenly. Put the pan in the freezer.

WHILE THE TOPPING FREEZES, MAKE THE CAKE BATTER

In a small bowl, stir together the flour, baking powder, and baking soda.

In the bowl of a stand mixer fitted with the paddle attachment, cream the butter and sugar on medium speed until light and fluffy, about 5 minutes. Add the orange zest, vanilla, and salt. While the mixer is running, add the eggs one at a time, beating well after each addition. Add about one-third of the flour mixture, then add half the buttermilk, followed by another one-third of the flour, then the remaining buttermilk, and finally the remaining flour.

Remove the pan from the freezer and, working quickly now to keep the caramel cold, arrange the plums cut-side down in a single layer on top of the frozen caramel. Pour the batter over the plums, gently smoothing it out without disturbing

the fruit. Bake for about 55 minutes, until a toothpick inserted three-quarters of the way into the cake comes out with no uncooked batter stuck to it.

Let cool in the pan, then run a butter knife around the edge and invert the cake onto a serving plate.

Store, loosely wrapped (because it's kind of gooey), at room temperature for up to 2 days or in the refrigerator for 3 to 4 days.

NOTE ON CAKE PAN SIZE
Do not attempt to bake this in a standard 8- or 9-inch (20- or 23-cm) cake pan—it will overflow. I know because I've tried, twice.

PEAR-GINGER VARIATION

Try making this cake with pear and ginger instead of plums. To do so, leave out the orange zest and add 2 teaspoons grated fresh ginger to the cake batter at the same time as the vanilla. Fan out thinly sliced pear in place of the plums, and scatter chopped candied ginger over the fruit before pouring in the cake batter.

BLOOD ORANGE VARIATION

You could also choose to make this an upside-down blood orange cake. For that option, use only ½ cup (120 ml) buttermilk and add ¼ cup (60 ml) fresh blood orange juice. Cut away the peel and white pith of 3 blood oranges, then slice the oranges into thin rounds and remove and discard the seeds. Arrange the fruit in a closely packed single layer on top of the frozen caramel.

Meet the critic, Liam Waldman

Sticky toffee whole-wheat date cake

Sticky toffee whole-wheat date cake

One day, Meadow made this and I lost my mind.

Makes 1 (8-inch/20-cm square or 9-inch/23-cm round) cake; serves 9 (V)

FOR THE CAKE

12 pitted dates (8 ounces/225 g total), chopped
1 tablespoon fresh lemon juice
½ cup (70 g) dried currants
1 cup (125 g) whole-wheat flour
½ cup plus 2 tablespoons (80 g) all-purpose
   flour
1 teaspoon baking soda
1 teaspoon ground cinnamon
½ teaspoon ground cardamom
¼ teaspoon ground ginger
¾ teaspoon fine sea salt

14 tablespoons (1¾ sticks/200 g) unsalted
   butter, at room temperature, plus more for
   the pan
¾ cup (165 g) packed brown sugar
2 large eggs
½ teaspoon vanilla extract

FOR THE STICKY TOFFEE

½ cup (170 g) agave nectar
½ cup (110 g) packed brown sugar
¼ teaspoon fine sea salt
2 tablespoons unsalted butter
Fleur de sel

MAKE THE CAKE

Preheat the oven to 325°F (165°C). Butter an 8-inch (20-cm) square or 9-inch (23-cm) round cake pan.

In a small pot, combine the dates, lemon juice, and ¾ cup (180 ml) water. Simmer gently until the dates soften and fall apart, about 6 minutes. Add the currants to the pot, then set aside to cool.

While the date mixture cools, stir together the whole-wheat flour, all-purpose flour, baking soda, cinnamon, cardamom, ginger, and salt.

Using a stand mixer fitted with the paddle attachment or electric beaters, beat the butter and brown sugar together on medium speed until light, 3 to 5 minutes. Add the eggs one at a time, mixing well after each addition and scraping down the sides of the bowl as needed. Mix in the vanilla and the cooled date mixture, followed by the flour mixture.

Scrape the batter into the prepared pan, spreading evenly and smoothing the surface. Bake for about 45 minutes, until a toothpick inserted into the center comes out clean with just a few crumbs clinging to it.

MEANWHILE, MAKE THE STICKY TOFFEE

In a small pot (you can use the same one you used for the dates, if it's still around), combine the agave, brown sugar, and salt. Bring to a simmer over medium heat, whisking to dissolve the sugar. Once it bubbles, remove from the heat and swirl in the butter.

When the cake comes out of the oven, spoon half the sticky toffee over it and let cool in the pan on a wire rack.

When the cake has cooled completely and the remaining sticky toffee has thickened, spread it over the cake. Sprinkle with fleur de sel and serve. Store, loosely wrapped, at room temperature for up to 2 days.

Cardamom doughnut-ish tea cakes

I know there are a lot of challenging recipes in this book. Here's one that's not. But don't be fooled by how straightforward it is. These tea cakes are one of our biggest crowd-pleasers.

Makes 12 (V)

FOR THE TEA CAKES

10 tablespoons (1¼ sticks/150 g) unsalted butter, melted, plus more for the muffin tin
2 cups (255 g) all-purpose flour
⅔ cup (135 g) sugar
2½ teaspoons baking powder
½ teaspoon baking soda
1 teaspoon ground cardamom
¾ teaspoon fine sea salt
1 large egg
1 cup (240 ml) whole milk

FOR THE CINNAMON-SUGAR TOPPING

⅓ cup (65 g) sugar
1 teaspoon ground cinnamon
¼ teaspoon ground cardamom
Pinch of fine sea salt
Unsalted butter, melted

MAKE THE TEA CAKES

Preheat the oven to 350°F (175°C). Butter just the bottom surface (not the sides) of a 12-well muffin tin.

In a large bowl, whisk together the flour, sugar, baking powder, baking soda, cardamom, and salt.

In another bowl, crack in the egg and whisk to break it up. Gradually whisk in the melted butter and milk.

Pour into the flour mixture, stirring just until combined. (If the batter looks lumpy and slightly under-mixed, it's perfect.)

Scoop the batter into each well of the muffin tin, filling them only three-quarters full. Bake until the tops are very light golden brown and spring back when you press on them, about 25 minutes. Let cool for a few minutes in the tins.

MEANWHILE, MAKE THE CINNAMON-SUGAR TOPPING

Stir together the sugar, cinnamon, cardamom, and salt. Once the tea cakes have cooled off a little, turn them out of the tins. Dip the tops into melted butter, then into the cinnamon sugar. Any bald patches can be brushed with melted butter and dipped into the sugar again.

These are best eaten immediately but can be stored, covered, overnight.

Pecan frangipane and rhubarb tarts

This is probably the most involved recipe in the desserts chapter. It has multiple components, but each one is pretty simple, as are all the techniques. However, if assembling little tarts made of graham cracker crust, pecan frangipane, and brown butter–coated rhubarb doesn't sound like your idea of a good time, then flip back to page 231 and try the Cardamom Doughnut-ish Tea Cakes.

Makes 12 (3-inch/7.5-cm) tarts (V)

FOR THE GRAHAM CRACKER CRUST

6 tablespoons (¾ stick/85 g) unsalted butter
14 (2½ by 5–inch/6 by 12–cm) graham
  crackers (recipe follows, or use store-bought)
  (7 ounces/200 g total)
½ cup (90 g) lightly packed brown sugar
½ teaspoon fine sea salt

FOR THE PECAN FRANGIPANE

¾ cup (75 g) pecans, toasted
½ cup (100 g) granulated sugar

⅓ cup (90 g) almond paste
½ teaspoon fine sea salt
½ cup (1 stick/115 g) unsalted butter, at room
  temperature
1 large egg
1 large egg yolk
1½ teaspoons dark rum

FOR THE RHUBARB AND TOPPING

1 small red rhubarb stalk, trimmed
Granulated sugar
Fleur de sel

MAKE THE GRAHAM CRACKER CRUST

Preheat the oven to 375°F (190°C).

Brown the butter in a small skillet. Set 1 tablespoon of the browned butter aside for the rhubarb.

In the bowl of a food processor fitted with a metal blade, combine the graham crackers, brown sugar, and salt. Pulse until the crackers have turned into crumbs. Pour in the 5 tablespoons (25 ml) browned butter and pulse to incorporate.

Spoon about 2 heaping tablespoons of the graham cracker mixture into each well of a muffin tin. Use the back of a small spoon to press the crumbs along the bottom and sides of the wells to create an even crust. You might have a few crumbs left over; use them to patch any thin parts in the crust. Bake for 8 to 10 minutes, until just the slightest bit darker around the edges.

As soon as you remove the muffin tin from the oven, use the back of the spoon to gently press any parts of the crust that look loose. Let cool completely. Engage all your will-power to not just stop here and eat the crust alone.

MAKE THE PECAN FRANGIPANE

In the bowl of a food processor fitted with a metal blade, grind the pecans and 2 teaspoons of the sugar to a fine meal. Using a stand mixer fitted with the paddle attachment, beat the remaining sugar, the almond paste, and salt on medium speed for 1 to 2 minutes, until the almond paste has crumbled and combined with the sugar. Add the butter, little by little, and continue beating for 3 minutes, stopping the mixer and scraping down the sides as needed. Add the egg and egg yolk and beat until fully incorporated, then mix in the ground pecans and rum.

ASSEMBLE THE RHUBARB TARTS

Preheat the oven to 350°F (175°C).

Cut the rhubarb stalk into ⅛-inch (3-mm) cubes. There should be about ¼ cup (30 g). Toss with the reserved 1 tablespoon browned butter.

Dollop a small spoonful of frangipane into each little graham cracker crust. Divide the rhubarb cubes evenly among the crusts, centering the fruit as best you can. Top with the remaining frangipane, about 2 teaspoons per tart. Sprinkle lightly with sugar and a pinch of fleur de sel. Bake for 20 to 25 minutes, until puffed and very light golden brown.

Let the tarts cool to room temperature in the muffin tin. Once cool, a narrow butter knife makes removing them from the tin slightly less difficult.

These are best eaten the day they are baked but can be stored, covered, at room temperature for another day or two.

Graham crackers

Here you go, just in case there weren't already enough steps for you in the frangipane tart recipe above.

Makes 16 (2½ by 5–inch/6 by 12–cm) crackers (V)

3 cups (360 g) graham flour **(see Note)**
1 cup (220 g) packed brown sugar
1 teaspoon baking soda
½ teaspoon ground cinnamon
1 teaspoon fine sea salt
½ cup (1 stick/115 g) unsalted butter, cut into
    pieces and chilled
¼ cup whole milk
¼ cup honey
2 teaspoons vanilla extract

In a large bowl, combine the graham flour, brown sugar, baking soda, cinnamon, and salt. Using your fingertips, quickly pinch and smash the butter into the flour mixture until it resembles pebbly sand. Stir in the milk, honey, and vanilla, stopping as soon as they are incorporated. Divide the stiff dough into two equal pieces, wrap in plastic, and place in the refrigerator to chill for at least 1 hour.

Preheat the oven to 375°F (190°C). Line two baking sheets with parchment paper.

On a well-floured surface, roll out the dough to 1/16 inch (2 mm) thick. Cut into 2½ by 5–inch (6 by 12–cm) rectangles, prick with a fork, and place on the prepared baking sheets, spacing them at least 1 inch (2.5 cm) apart. Bake, rotating the position of the baking sheets at the midway point, until lightly browned around the edges, 15 minutes. Let cool on the baking sheets.

Store in an airtight container at room temperature for up to 5 days.

NOTE ON GRAHAM FLOUR
We buy ours from Anson Mills. Bob's Red Mill also sells it, as does King Arthur.

Lemon verbena peach pie

Lemon verbena peach pie

Meadow has a thing for pie. Whenever she makes one at Sqirl, she posts a picture of it on Instagram and our regulars call in asking us to hold a piece for them. This is how she lures people into the space. By people, I mean men. I didn't know pie was an aphrodisiac, but apparently it is right up there with oysters.

Makes 1 (9-inch/23-cm) pie; serves 8 (V)

FOR THE FILLING

1⅓ cups (265 g) sugar
1 bunch (60 g) fresh lemon verbena
6 to 8 peaches (2 pounds 14 ounces/1.3 kg total), pitted and sliced
3 tablespoons cornstarch
¼ cup (60 ml) fresh lemon juice
Fine sea salt

FOR THE CRUST

1 large egg
2⅔ cups (335 g) all-purpose flour
2 teaspoons sugar, plus more for sprinkling
¾ teaspoon fine sea salt
1⅓ cups (2⅔ sticks/300 g) unsalted butter, chilled and cut into cubes
Heavy cream

MAKE THE FILLING

Combine the sugar and 1 cup (240 ml) water in a large pot. Bring to a simmer, stirring to dissolve the sugar. Add the lemon verbena and cook for 3 minutes at a gentle simmer. Add half the peaches and cook, stirring often, until they soften and look a little more vibrant, about 10 minutes.

Strain the cooked peaches and syrup through a fine-mesh sieve, catching all the syrup in a bowl. Pour the strained syrup back into the pot. Set the cooked peaches aside and pick out and discard the lemon verbena. Cook the syrup at a brisk simmer until it reduces in volume by half, 8 to 10 minutes. Add the remaining raw peaches, followed by the cooked peaches, and cook just until the raw peaches begin to soften, about 8 minutes.

Meanwhile, in a small bowl, combine the cornstarch, lemon juice, and a pinch of salt, stirring until there are no lumps.

Once the raw peaches begin to soften, add the cornstarch slurry to the pot and cook, stirring continuously, until the liquid thickens, about 20 seconds. Pour the filling into a heat-resistant container, cover, and chill in the refrigerator until completely cold (see Note).

MAKE THE DOUGH

Measure ¼ cup (60 ml) cold water in a glass. Crack in the egg and stir well. Put the glass in the freezer to chill.

In a large bowl, combine the flour, sugar, and salt. Using your fingertips, quickly pinch and smash the butter into the flour mixture. Once there are no butter pieces larger than a pea, drizzle in the egg-and-ice-water mixture. Still working quickly, toss to incorporate the water, then turn the dough out onto a cutting board and shape it into two disks, one slightly bigger than the other. Wrap the disks in plastic and put them in the fridge to chill for at least 2 hours. (The dough can be made up to 2 days in advance.)

On a lightly floured surface, roll out the bigger disk to a 13-inch (33-cm) circle and set it inside a 9-inch (23-cm) pie dish, letting the edges hang over the sides of the dish. Place in the fridge to chill while you roll out the smaller disk to an 11-inch

(28-cm) circle. Remove the pie dish from the fridge and pour in the chilled filling. Arrange the top crust over the filling.

Now you're going to roll and crimp the overhanging edges of the crust. Using your thumb and pointer finger, pinch the top and bottom layers together and roll them under themselves so they form a double-thick edge that perches along the rim of the dish. Once you've rolled around the entire crust, use two pointer fingers and a thumb to crimp the edge, pressing the dough between your fin-

gers every 1 inch (2.5 cm) or so. Cut a ring of slits around the center for steam to escape while the pie bakes. Put the pie in the freezer to chill and preheat the oven to 400°F (205°C).

Brush the crust with cream and sprinkle evenly with sugar. Set the dish on a rimmed baking sheet to catch any drips. Bake for 10 minutes, then adjust the oven temperature to 350°F (175°C) and bake for another 1 hour 15 minutes to 1 hour 25 minutes. (Yes, really that long!) When the pie is done, the filling will be bubbling slowly through the mid-

dle vent and the crust will be nice and deep, dark brown. Let cool for at least 4 hours before serving.

Store, tightly wrapped, at room temperature for up to 2 days. If you like, you can reheat the pie in a 325°F (160°C) oven until warm.

CHILLING THE FILLING
It's important the filling be completely cold when you assemble the pie, otherwise the crust won't hold up.

NOTE ON CRUST
This crust is a friend to any pie filling.

Lemon verbena peach pie

Register now for Nathan Cozzolino's three-day pastry intake seminar

Drinks
238—
259

Sqirl doesn't have a liquor license, which means we'd better find another way to make our drinks enticing. We could offer just drip coffee and lattes, but where's the fun in that? We've chosen to experiment with drinks in much the same way that we play around with the food. While some additions to our menu came about organically (we have rice and make almond milk, so why not make horchata?), others happened as a result of our experiences in the wild West. Here's a puzzle for you: What's juice-centric, non-caffeinated, and detoxifying? If you answered turmeric tonic, you'd be correct.

Brown rice horchata

Brown rice horchata

Since the early days of Sqirl, I've wanted to serve horchata. It was an obvious drink for us to make because we have both homemade almond milk and really good rice. For a while, different guys on the night crew tried making horchata. I wanted it to be good enough that David Prado, who was born in Tecuala in the Mexican state of Nayarit and who is also the head of the night crew, wanted to drink it. We played around with the recipe until one day he tasted it and said, "Okay, close enough."

Makes 1 quart (960 ml); serves 6 (GF, VV)

1 cinnamon stick
½ cup (100 g) medium-grain brown rice
Scant 1½ cups (200 g) raw whole almonds
½ cup (100 g) pitted Medjool dates (about 6)
Pinch of fine sea salt
4¾ cups (1.1 L) boiling water
Ground cinnamon

Toast the cinnamon stick in a dry pan over medium-low heat for about 5 minutes. You want all those fragrant oils to come out. After 5 minutes or so, your home should smell like a cinnamon stick factory. Don't worry if the cinnamon burns; I'm not offended by the burn.

In a large bowl, combine the rice, almonds, dates, and salt. Pick up the toasted cinnamon stick (be careful—it's probably still hot), break it into small pieces, and add to the bowl. Pour in the boiling water. Let the mixture sit until it has cooled to room temperature, about 4 hours.

Transfer everything in the bowl to a high-speed blender. Blend, starting on the lowest setting and increasing the speed steadily. Strain through a nut-milk bag suspended over a bowl, squeezing to collect all the liquid.

Serve over ice, with a sprinkling of ground cinnamon on top—oh, so fancy!

Store, covered, in the refrigerator for 2 days. On the third day, shake it, smell it, and make the decision.

HORCHOFFEE
At Sqirl we started making something we call horchoffee that has become loved by both our cooks and our customers. To make a single serving, pour 1 generous cup (270 ml) of horchata into a cocktail shaker filled with ice cubes. Add a double shot of espresso, shake well, then pour into a glass with just a few ice cubes. Sprinkle ground cinnamon on top. If you don't have espresso at home (only the very lucky do), then you can substitute about 2 tablespoons undiluted cold-brewed coffee concentrate (page 249). However, it won't really be the same; espresso is far superior. The sweetness of espresso crema makes it such that we don't need to add any additional sweeteners. But if cold-brewed coffee is what you've got, it's still worth a shot.

Cascara tea

This doesn't really taste anything like coffee, even though it's made from coffee cherries, which are the fruits of the plant. It tastes like hibiscus, has only one-quarter the caffeine level of coffee, and is just delicious.

Makes 1 quart (1 L); serves 6 (GF, VV)

½ cup (20 g) dried coffee cherries (available online from 49th Parallel)
4 cups (950 ml) filtered water

Put the coffee cherries in a 1-quart (1-L) jar and pour in the cold water. Cover the jar with a piece of plastic wrap (because jar lids go missing like socks in the wash). Let steep in the refrigerator for 12 hours.

Strain and enjoy over ice.

NOTE ON COLD BREW VS. HOT BREW
You could, of course, brew this tea hot. That's how it's enjoyed in coffee-producing parts of the world. In LA, though, we usually crave it iced.

Lait 'n' egg

One of Sqirl's early employees, Mike Lockwood, returned from a trip to Vietnam and kept talking about *cà phê trứng* Vietnamese coffee made with whipped egg yolk. This of course got us all inspired to play around and figure out how to make a version of that drink at Sqirl. Instead of yolks, we went down the whites path and decided to froth them in a cocktail shaker.

Serves 2 or 3 (GF, VV)

FOR THE COLD-BREWED COFFEE CONCENTRATE

¾ cup (60 g) coarsely ground coffee beans
1½ cups (360 ml) filtered water

FOR THE LAIT 'N' EGG

2 large egg whites
2 generous tablespoons organic sweetened
 condensed milk

MAKE THE COLD-BREWED COFFEE CONCENTRATE

Put the ground coffee in a jar, pour in the water, and stir gently. Cover and let steep in the refrigerator for 12 hours.

Strain the brew through a coffee filter set inside a funnel or a sieve. It'll take a few minutes for all the liquid to drip through the filter. You'll be tempted to help it drip faster, but just disappear. Go do something else. Go make popcorn. If you do force the liquid through, you'll end up with small particles in your cold-brewed coffee and it won't be nice and clear.

Now you have full-concentrate cold-brewed coffee. (Have any exams you need to study for?) Set aside ⅔ cup (165 ml). Enjoy the remaining cold-brewed coffee, diluted with an equal amount of cool, filtered water, over ice.

FOR THE LAIT 'N' EGG

In a small bowl, whisk the egg whites and condensed milk until fully combined. Fill a 24-ounce (720-ml) cocktail shaker with ice cubes. Pour in the egg-milk mixture and the cold-brewed coffee. Shake until nicely chilled and frothy, about 10 seconds. Pour everything—ice and all—into two or three small glasses.

NOTE ON BREWING COFFEE
If you're reaching for a French press, don't. That lid smells like old coffee. Just use a big, clean jar.

NOTE ON SCALING UP
You can easily scale up the amount of cold-brewed coffee, if you desire.

The amount of beans listed in this recipe will yield a little under 1 cup (240 ml) cold-brewed coffee concentrate, which is enough for 2 or 3 servings of Lait 'n' Egg. But if you want to have more cold-brewed coffee around to sip on all week or to share with friends, it takes almost no effort to brew a little extra. Just keep the ratio of beans to water the same. For example, to end up with 1 quart (960 ml) cold-brewed concentrate, use 3 cups (240 g) ground beans and 6 cups (1.4 L) water.

NOTE ON THE COFFEE BEANS
Save your freshest coffee beans for hot coffee opportunities. Cold-brewed coffee is great when it's made with less-than-fresh beans. It's fine to collect all the different kinds of coffee beans in your kitchen and combine them for this recipe.

Orange-vanilla soda

Here's a recipe you can easily double or triple to make a big batch. Keep this soda in your fridge on a hot summer day and invite ~~me~~ some friends over.

Makes 1 quart (960 ml); serves 6 (GF, VV)

½ cup (100 g) sugar
¼ teaspoon citric acid
4 or 5 Valencia oranges
½ vanilla bean
Sparkling water

In a pot, combine ½ cup (120 ml) water with the sugar, citric acid, and the finely grated zest of 1 orange. Slice the vanilla bean in half lengthwise and use the dull edge of your knife to scrape all the tiny black seeds into a little pile on your cutting board. Drop the scraped bean into the pot. Simmer the syrup, stirring once or twice, for about 15 minutes. Turn off the heat, then stir in the vanilla seeds. You will have to use your arm muscles to whisk and break up the clusters of seeds. Let cool completely, then strain through a fine-mesh sieve and discard the zest.

Fill six tall glasses with ice cubes. Squeeze 1½ cups (360 ml) juice from the oranges. Pour ¼ cup (60 ml) of the juice and 1 table-spoon of the orange-vanilla syrup into each glass. (You will have a little syrup left over; you can use it to further sweeten the soda, if you like.) Add enough sparkling water to fill each glass. Stir with a long metal spoon and enjoy.

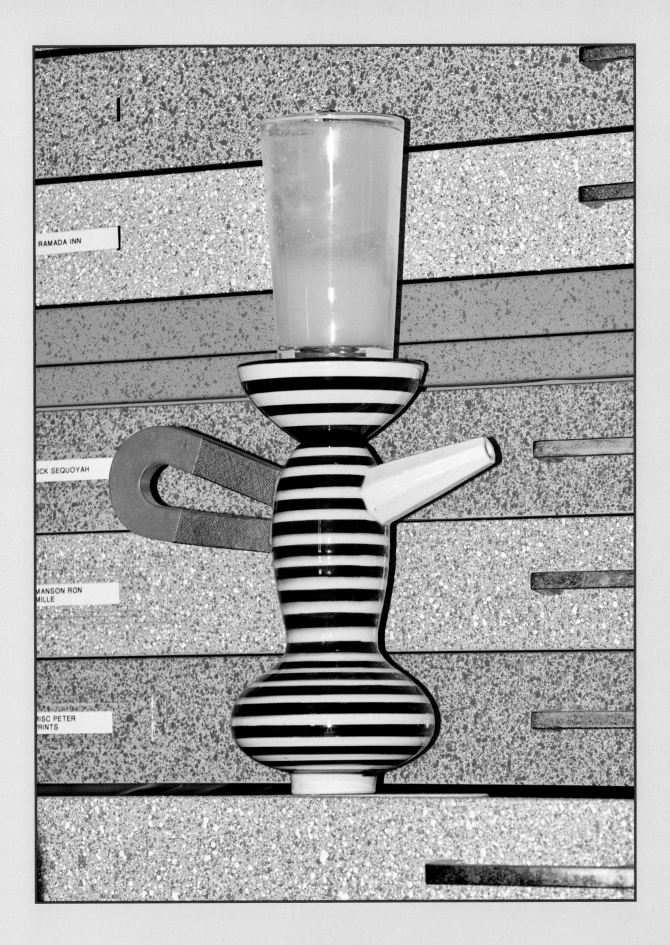

Rhubarb lemonade

Who runs the world? Sqirls.

Makes 1 quart (1 L); serves 6 (GF, VV)

1⅓ cups (200 g) chopped rhubarb
⅔ cup (135 g) sugar
½ cup plus 1 tablespoon (135 ml) fresh lemon
  juice (from about 3 lemons)

Put the rhubarb, sugar, and 1⅔ cups (400 ml) water in a pot. Bring to a boil, then reduce the heat so that the syrup simmers. Cook for about 20 minutes, stirring every once in a while, until the rhubarb has fallen apart and imbued the liquid with its color.

While the syrup is still hot, pour it through a fine-mesh sieve into a large measuring cup or bowl. Use a rubber spatula to really press on the rhubarb mush and squeeze out every last drop. Let cool.

There should be about 1¼ cups (300 ml) rhubarb syrup. (If there is more, save it for adding later on. My palate loves a good amount of acid, so you may want to use the extra syrup to increase the sweetness to your liking.) Pour the rhubarb syrup into a 1-quart (1-L) jar. Add the lemon juice and 2 cups plus 1 table-spoon (495 ml) water. Screw on the jar's lid and shake well.

Serve chilled over ice.

NOTE ON RHUBARB
At Sqirl we use up the knobby ends of rhubarb stalks that get skipped over when we make strawberry-rhubarb and blue-barb jam.

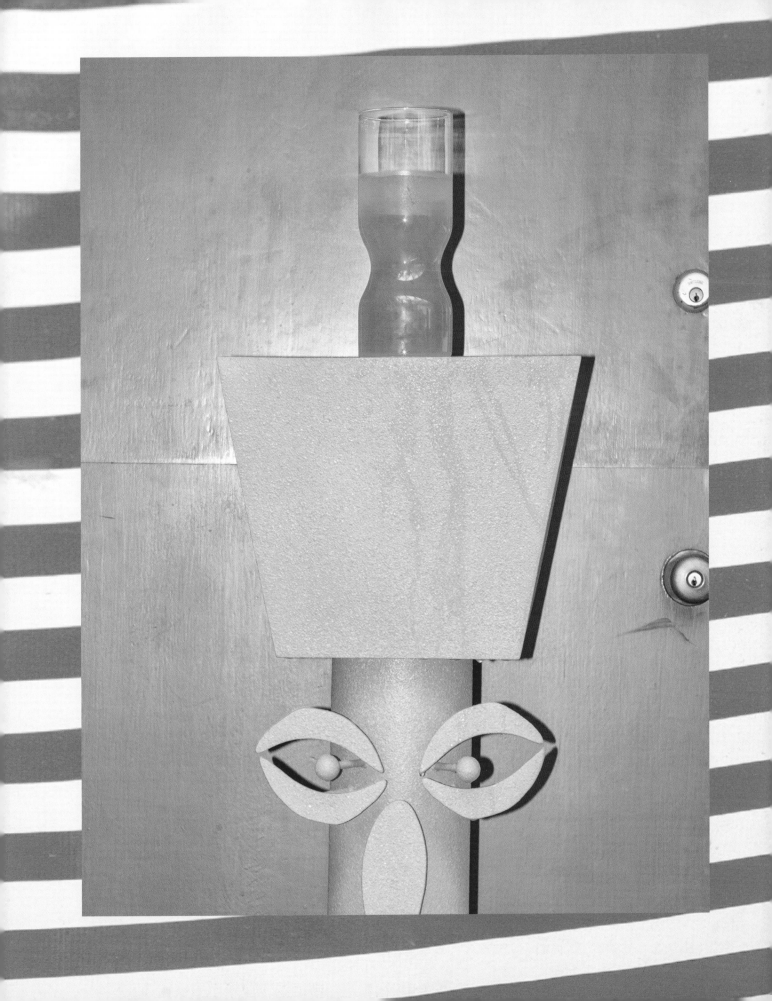

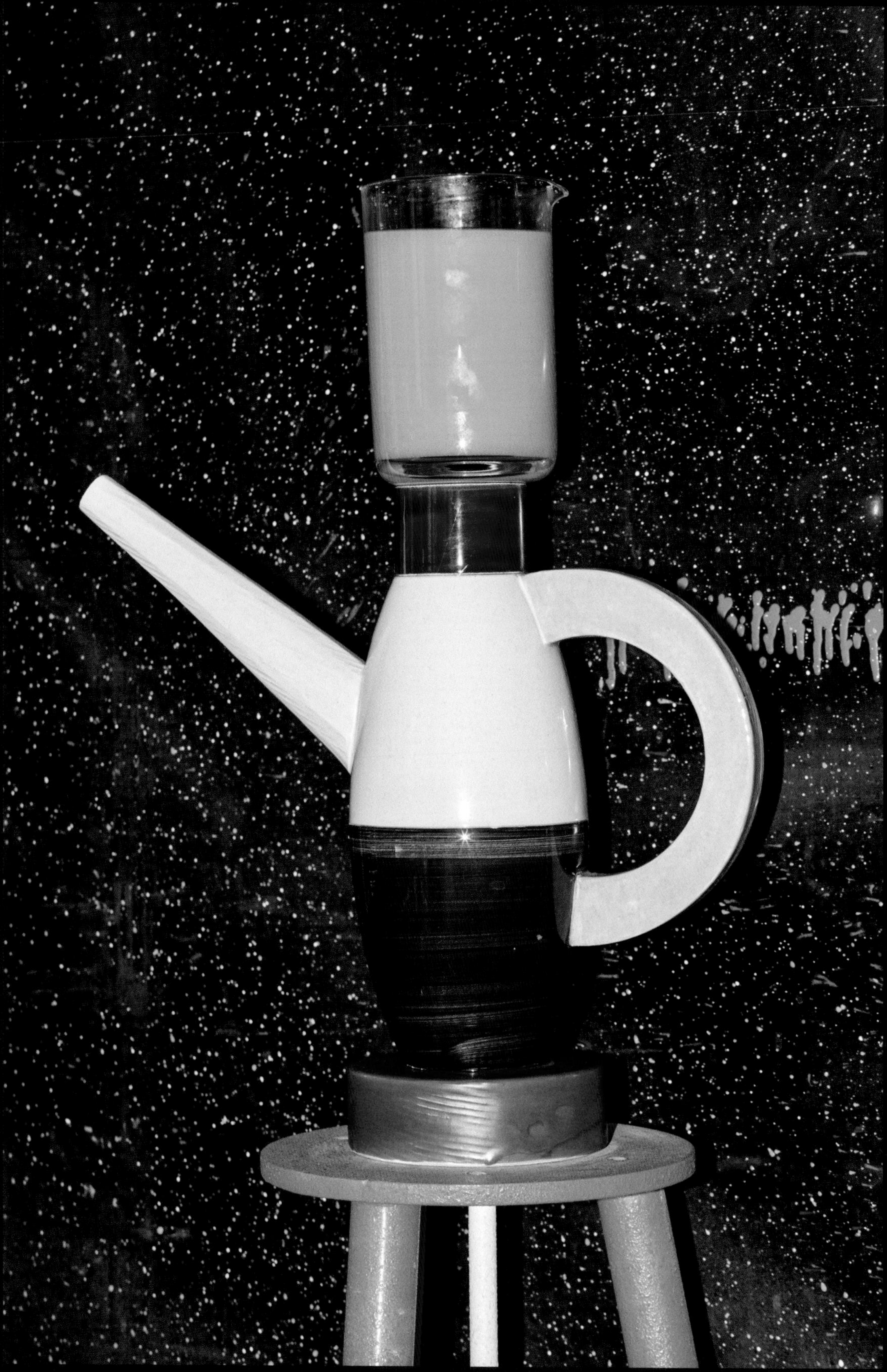

Turmeric tonic

Avocado cardamom smoothie

This recipe was inspired by the avocado ice cream served on toasted milk bread at Morgenstern's in NYC, which was probably inspired by a classic Vietnamese avocado shake (*sinh tố bơ*). I wanted to turn those rich flavors into something I could have every day.

Serves 2, with some left over, like a milkshake (GF, VV)

½ teaspoon whole cardamom seeds (the little
    black things inside the green pods, not the
    pods themselves)
1 ripe Hass avocado
⅔ cup (160 ml) organic sweetened condensed milk
2 cups ice cubes
1 tablespoon high-quality extra-virgin olive oil
    (optional)
Fleur de sel (optional)

In a small, dry pan over medium-low heat, toast the cardamom seeds for about 4 minutes, stirring every so often so they don't burn. Transfer the seeds to a cutting board and use the back of a spoon to crush them to a powder.

Halve and pit the avocado, then scrape both halves of the avocado flesh into a high-speed blender and discard the peel.

Pour in the condensed milk and ¾ cup (180 ml) water. Add the ice cubes and ¼ teaspoon of the ground cardamom. Turn on the machine, starting on the lowest setting and increasing the speed steadily. Blend for about 20 seconds. Turn off the blender and use a rubber spatula to check that the ice has been blended. If it has not, stir and then blend for another 10 seconds, starting on the lowest setting and increasing the speed steadily. Taste the smoothie

and decide if you want to add more ground cardamom. (I always want to add more cardamom.)

Pour into two tall glasses. If you like, drizzle about ½ tablespoon oil into each glass and finish with a pinch of fleur de sel.

NOTE ON CONDENSED MILK
Don't wuss out and get nonorganic condensed milk; that stuff is gross.

Lactose Free? Be happy with housemade Almond Milk.

Larder

260— 269

These sauces, dressings, and other pantry items can always be found in the Sqirl kitchen. Though they are small components, they make a big impact when added to dishes, turning the usual into the memorable. Some, like Crème Fraîche (page 265) and Fermented Jalapeño Hot Sauce (page 267), are utilized in many recipes throughout this book. Others don't have specific recipes to which they are linked, and can be used in a variety of ways. I'll leave that up to you because you will find out on your own that the Green Goddess Dressing (page 266) is delicious tossed with leafy salad greens. Look for additional larder-type recipes in other chapters—the Preserved Meyer Lemons (page 64) deserve a home in your home, as do the Pickled Carrots (page 48).

Crème Fraîche

Ricotta

Aioli

If you come to Sqirl, there's an off-menu sandwich during tomato season you should know about called the $20 BLT. It actually started as a dish that all our cooks would eat when they were taking their breaks. After working for probably five hours, you're craving something hearty. So this sandwich is what one of our chefs started making for everyone, and it just stuck.

We take thick slices of buttered and toasted brioche and slather them on one side with aioli. Then we put ripe slices of tomato on top of the aioli, season them with salt and pepper, and put three or four pieces of crisp house-made bacon (page 115) on top of that. Finally, we stack some really fresh, vibrant lettuce on top. It's a lot, but it actually tastes surprisingly light and doesn't feel as heavy as you might imagine.

Makes about ¾ cup (170 g) (GF, V)

1 to 2 cloves garlic
½ teaspoon fine sea salt, or more to taste
1 large egg yolk
½ cup (120 ml) extra-virgin olive oil
½ cup (120 ml) non-GMO canola oil
½ lemon (optional)

Using a mortar and pestle, smash the garlic and salt together until smooth. Add the egg yolk, then pound with the pestle to break up the yolk.

Combine the olive oil and canola oil in a measuring cup that has a pouring spout. While stirring the garlic-egg mixture with the pestle, slowly drizzle in a few drops of the blended oil. Keep stirring in the same direction as you add another few drops. You'll notice the aioli will begin to emulsify; it will thicken and get sticky. Once it gets ribbony and tight, you may want to add a squeeze of lemon juice to loosen it up, although you don't have to.

Stay with this tempo, stirring and very, very slowly adding the oil, until you've added it all. It's important to drizzle in the oil in a slow, steady stream, and it's also important to stir continuously but not too fast. It helps if a friend holds the mortar so that it doesn't move around on your countertop. You can also put a damp towel underneath.

Once you've added all the oil, taste the aioli and add a bit more salt, if it needs it. You can squeeze in a little lemon juice to give it some acidity, or you can just leave it as is.

Aioli is best the day it is made.

NOTE ON EMULSIFICATION

Sometimes when you try to make aioli, it breaks. You'll know because the oil will separate from the yolk and the whole thing will look thin and not gloppy like mayonnaise. To fix this, crack a fresh egg yolk into a clean bowl. Transfer the broken aioli to a container that has a pouring spout. While stirring the new yolk, slowly—very, very slowly—add the broken aioli drop by drop, treating it as if it were the oil. You may need to add more oil after you've added all the broken aioli because now you're working with two yolks.

NOTE ON TOOLS

It's possible to make aioli using a bowl and a whisk, or a food processor with a pour spout, or even an immersion blender. For the food processor, it'll work better if you double or even triple this recipe; one yolk isn't quite enough volume for the spinning blade to reach successfully.

Almond hazelnut butter

We make a lot of nut butter at the restaurant using a large countertop nut mill. Our food processors at home are never going to grind nut butter that's quite the same. It'll be thinner. It'll take longer to turn into nut butter. It will get stiff over time (but with a good elbow you can bring it back). And the food processor is going to get hot and bothered in the process. So find a jar of nut butter or you can try making your own at home. You can play around with the proportions of almonds and hazelnuts. As a starting point, here's how we like it best.

Makes about 2 cups (520 g) (GF, VV)

2 cups (280 g) whole almonds, roasted and
    chopped
1 cup (135 g) whole hazelnuts, roasted and
    chopped
Non-GMO canola oil, as needed
Fine sea salt (optional)

Put the nuts in the bowl of a food processor fitted with a metal blade. Process for 1 minute, then stop the machine and scrape down the sides of the bowl. The mixture should look like it is on its way toward becoming nut butter: finely chopped, not solid but not really liquid either, and starting to clump. If the nuts are having a hard time turning into nut butter, add 1 teaspoon of oil. Blend for 2 minutes. Stop the machine, let it cool off, and scrape down the sides of the bowl. At this point, the nut butter should look pretty smooth and thick. Try to avoid adding any more oil. Blend for 1 final minute.

At Sqirl we don't usually salt our nut butter because we're always spreading it across brioche toast and sprinkling it with a heavy pinch of fleur de sel (page 39). I'll leave the salting up to you.

The nut butter will be warm from the friction. Pour into a heat resistant containerand let it sit in your pantry for 1 day. As it cools to room temperature, it will firm up, although it may still be a little thinner than you are used to. Store in a jar at room temperature for up to 3 months.

Almond milk

I love a recipe that requires time that you don't have to be present for. Go do something else while the mixture cools.

Makes about 3 cups (720 ml) (GF, VV)

1⅔ cups (235 g) whole blanched almonds
2 tablespoons sugar
Pinch of fine sea salt
3⅓ cups (790 ml) boiling water

In a medium bowl, combine the almonds, sugar, and salt. Pour in the water—it must be absolutely boiling hot. Let the mixture sit until it has cooled to room temperature, about 3 hours.

Blend in a high-speed blender. Pour through a nut-milk bag suspended over a bowl, then squeeze the bag to collect all the almond milk.

Store, covered, in the refrigerator for up to 3 days. It doesn't have a long shelf life, so drink it!

SUGAR-FREE VARIATION
Swap the sugar for 2 pitted dates.

Crème fraîche

I like to whip crème fraîche to give it some nice texture. You can whisk by hand or use electric beaters. Look for the moment when the crème fraîche changes from glossy to matte—that's when it's done. Just as with whipped cream, when you lift out the beaters, the whipped crème fraîche should stand up in soft peaks.

Makes about 2 cups (480 ml) (GF, V)

2 cups (480 ml) heavy cream
1½ teaspoons cultured buttermilk (not ultrapasteurized)

In a nonreactive container, combine the cream and buttermilk. Cover and leave out at room temperature for 24 to 36 hours, until slightly thickened. If it's a warm day, the cream will thicken a little faster than it would on a cool day. We usually write the time on a piece of tape and stick it to the container because it's easy to forget when you started.

Stir and place in the refrigerator, where it will thicken further as it chills. Crème fraîche will keep in the refrigerator for up to 2 weeks.

Everyday mustard vinaigrette

This is our dressing for all side salads at the restaurant. We leave it mellow and perhaps even a bit underseasoned so that when we're making the salad, we have the freedom to add a little more salt or lemon juice, depending on how the greens taste that day.

Makes about 1½ cups (360 ml) (GF, VV)

2 tablespoons plus 2 teaspoons brown or yellow mustard seeds
½ teaspoon sugar
¼ cup (60 ml) white wine vinegar
1 cup (240 ml) extra-virgin olive oil
2 tablespoons fresh lemon juice
Fine sea salt and freshly ground black pepper

First, make mustard: In a bowl or jar, combine the mustard seeds, sugar, vinegar, and ¼ cup (60 ml) water. Cover and let sit for 3 days at room temperature. It's not a problem if you let the mustard seeds soak for a day or two longer, but they do need at least 72 hours to soften.

Pour the soaked mustard seeds and liquid into the bowl of a blender or food processor fitted with a metal blade. Blend on high speed until smooth.

Next, turn the mustard into mustard vinaigrette: While the machine is running, gradually pour in ½ cup (120 ml) of the oil, then add the lemon juice and ¼ teaspoon salt, followed by the remaining ½ cup (120 ml) oil. Season with more salt and pepper to taste. The vinaigrette will keep, covered, in the refrigerator for at least 1 week.

Southern-style fresh cream and black mustard dressing

Don't let the word *cream* deter you from making this dressing. It's light, and a little goes a long way.

Makes about 1 cup (240 ml) (GF, V)

1 tablespoon minced shallot (½ small)
1 teaspoon black mustard seeds
2 tablespoons white wine vinegar
Fine sea salt
½ cup (120 ml) heavy cream

In a small bowl, combine the shallot, mustard seeds, vinegar, and ¼ teaspoon salt. Let soften for 15 minutes.

In another bowl, whip the cream. You'll probably need to whisk by hand because it's such a small amount of cream. It should form medium-soft peaks and double in size. (If you're making a double batch, you can use electric beaters to make your life easier.)

Using a rubber spatula, fold the cream and softened shallot mixture together. Taste and adjust the seasoning, adding another pinch of salt, if needed. It'll keep, covered, in the refrigerator for a few days, though it loses its fluffiness as it sits.

Green goddess dressing

When you're not dressing salad with everyday mustard vinaigrette, use this green goddess dressing. Let's say you've got an avocado that's teetering on the far edge of ripe and you need to do something with it—fast. Have some leftover aioli lying around?

Makes about 2 cups (480 ml) (GF, V)

⅓ cup (80 ml) white wine vinegar
1 teaspoon honey
½ ripe Hass avocado, pitted and peeled
1 cup (50 g) loosely packed fresh flat-leaf
  parsley leaves (½ small bunch)
2 tablespoons chopped fresh chives
2 tablespoons fresh tarragon leaves
½ teaspoon fine sea salt, or more to taste
¾ cup aioli (page 263)

In the bowl of a food processor fitted with a metal blade, combine the vinegar, honey, avocado, parsley, chives, tarragon, salt, and ⅓ cup (80 ml) water. Blend until everything is well mixed but there are still big pieces of herb leaves. Transfer to a bowl, then fold in the aioli. Taste and add a little more salt, if it needs it.

Store in an airtight container in the fridge for up to 4 days.

Fermented jalapeño hot sauce

This hot sauce is lactofermented right up to the point when we boil it.

Makes about 2½ cups (600 ml) (GF, VV)

20 jalapeño peppers (1 pound/455 g total)
Fine sea salt or Diamond Crystal kosher salt, as
    needed **(see Note)**
1 cup (240 ml) distilled white vinegar

Cut the tops off the jalapeños, then slice each pepper in half lengthwise. Remove and discard the seeds. Chop the peppers into big pieces, put them in the bowl of a food processor fitted with a metal blade, and blend until mostly pureed but still a little bit chunky. Weigh the blended jalapeños, then use this equation to figure out exactly how much salt to add:

$$\text{grams of blended jalapeños} \times 0.075 = \text{grams of kosher salt}$$

Stir the salt into the blended jalapeños, then scrape the mash into a clean jar. (You'll need a jar that is slightly bigger than 1 pint/480 ml.)

Now choose a slightly smaller jar that will fit within the jar holding the jalapeño mash, weighing the mash down so it is fully submerged. Alternatively, if you don't have a smaller jar, make a brine using the same ratio of salt to water. So, for 480 ml (2 cups) water, you'll need to add 36 g/¼ cup of salt. Pour the brine into a plastic bag, get as much air out of the bag as possible, and then seal it well. Put the brine-filled bag directly on top of the mash in the jar, making sure the bag is covering the mash completely so that no air can get to the mixture. Label and date the jar, then let it sit in a dark, cool spot for 4 weeks.

Don't be afraid if you see white mold or some Kahm yeast growing on top of the mixture. Just skim it off and make sure the bag is still sealing the fermenting mixture from the air.

After 4 weeks, transfer the fermented pepper mixture to a nonreactive pot and stir in the vinegar. Bring to a boil. Remove from the heat, then carefully puree in a blender on high speed until uniform and saucy.

Store the fermented jalapeño hot sauce in an airtight container in the fridge. It will keep for at least 6 months.

NOTE ON SALT
Other brands of kosher salt can sometimes have anti-caking agents, which will interfere with fermentation. Check the package for additives.

Magic green sauce

Magic green sauce is really good swirled into pureed soups. Other green sauces worth checking out: Green Harissa (page 96), Mint Salsa Verde (page 107), and Cilantro Pistou (page 71).

Makes 2 to 3 cups (480 to 710 ml) (GF, VV)

3 cloves garlic
⅓ cup (80 ml) fresh lemon juice
1 teaspoon fine sea salt
1 bunch fresh flat-leaf parsley
1⅓ cups (300 ml) extra-virgin olive oil

Put the garlic in a high-speed blender and pour in the lemon juice. Add as much salt as you think the entire batch of green sauce will need. If you add the salt at the end, it won't dissolve easily and it'll mess with the vibrant green color, so that's why you have to sort of guess here. As a guide, we add 1 teaspoon.

Blend on low speed until the garlic is completely incorporated into the lemon juice.

Cut the whole bunch of parsley right at the point where the leaves start branching from the stems. Take the leafy top part and drop it into the blender. Blend on the lowest setting until the parsley starts catching on the spinning blade, about 10 seconds. Gradually increase the speed while you slowly pour in the oil. Once you've added all the oil, blend on high speed for 20 seconds. The sauce will be neon green and thick like mayonnaise.

It will keep, covered, in the refrigerator for a few days, but it might lose its neon green color.

Schmearable "ricotta"

Hey, I know this isn't true ricotta since it is made from milk, not whey. But don't let that stop you from making this rendition, which is fluffy and delicious and perfect for schmearing on toast.

Makes about 1½ cups (360 ml) (GF, V)

Scant ½ teaspoon citric acid **(see Note)**
4 cups (960 ml) whole milk
¾ cup (180 ml) heavy cream

Measure the citric acid into a tiny bowl, then add a splash of hot water (from the tap) and stir until the citric acid has completely dissolved.

Pour the milk into a nonreactive pot. Cook gently and slowly over low heat, stirring a few times with a rubber spatula, until the milk reaches 180°F (82°C), at which point you'll see it start to steam and look frothy around the edges of the pot. Remove from the heat, stir in the citric acid solution, then let rest for about 15 minutes or until you can press your hand against the side of the pot and keep it there comfortably for a few seconds.

Set up a straining station by nesting a fine-mesh sieve within a larger bowl. (If you don't have a fine-mesh sieve, you can use a colander with a piece of cheese-cloth draped across it.) Pour in the curdled milk and let it drain for 20 to 30 minutes. The longer you let it go, the thicker the ricotta will be. There's no need to weigh it down or squeeze it at all. The liquid that drips through is true whey. Keep it in your fridge and use it for all sorts of things: to jump-start lactofermented pickles, to marinate meat, to make biscuits, and even to fertilize plants!

Transfer the ricotta to a bowl. Fold in the cream, starting with just a little splash at first and then gradually adding as much of the remaining cream as needed. The point is to get it fluffy. If you add too much cream, it'll deflate the ricotta. If you don't add enough, you'll end up with chunky curds. Aim for thick but almost pourable.

Fresh ricotta goes bad fast. Store it, covered, in the refrigerator for a day or two. Use it up!

NOTE ON CITRIC ACID
It has such a powerful kick and provides that heavy zing that I love. Will the milk curdle with lemon juice? Yeah, but not the same way. Look for citric acid online.

Index

Sugar Sherm feeling the cool, Sqirl breeze

Acknowledgments

Thank you to all the customers who have made their way through our doors over the last half of a decade, and who continue to bring positivity and good energy to Sqirl. To those friends and Sqirl family who took time out of their days to come and sit for a portrait, thank you. I love you for those minutes. Vi Ha, I'm looking at you.

The same goes for my kitchen and FOH crew, past and present, who possess the openness to play and the rigidness to keep it tight, keep it right. Special thanks to: Meadow Ramsey, Javier Ramos, Royston Garza, David Prado, Patch Troffer, Jayme Darling, and Sara Storrie. Hands please.

To all the farmers, both in my heart and listed here: Robin and Ross Koda, Peter Schaner, Ron Cornelsen (RIP), Barbara and Bill Spencer, Kong Thao, Andy Mariani and Ken Brown, Steven and Robin Smith, Elizabeth Poett, Shu and Debby Takikawa, James Birch, Bill and Linda Zaiser, and Romeo Coleman. Thank you for honoring the land and letting us take your produce on a journey.

Thank you to everyone at Abrams who worked to bring this book to life. To Holly Dolce and Michael Sand, for believing in me from day one. Thank you to John Gall, Liam Flanagan, True Sims, Sarah Massey, Mary Hern, Liana Krissoff, Sally Knapp, Claire Bamundo, and Melissa Esner for being the crossers of all t's.

To Katherine Cowles, our shepherd! I feel so lucky to be under your discerning guidance. To Scott Barry,

I could not have done it without you. To see how far we've come is sometimes just incomprehensible. Wishing you Meyer lemons for life and sending love to Rich Barry for all eternity. To Peter Meehan, my east coast shoulder, like a great '80s suit with shoulder pads.

Thank you to Lynda Obst and Michael Krikorian for lending their words to this book. A huge thank you to Claire Cottrell, Jaime Beechum, and Nacho Alegre for giving this book a powerful visual narrative. And to Chris McElrath and all those at Contact Photo Lab who helped to develop a unifying tone. Cheers to that (with Laphroaig!). To Brooke Intrachat, thank you for managing, defining, and contributing talent. To Peter Shire, thanks for allowing us to shoot in your studio and home, for being a kingpin in this community, and for being true to your mind's work. You're a legend.

To Maria Zizka, for distilling Sqirl's essence while becoming a dear friend in the process. Love and thanks to Graham Bradley for his unwavering support.

A very special thank you to Anne Quatrano, for taking a chance on a kid who stared longingly into kitchens wishing she could be in one. You taught me teamwork, tough love, and to always stay true to my vision—no matter how challenging that may be. To Ryan Erlich, my rock, the most wonderful person I know in this life. Your support and love mean everything to me. And last but not least, thank you to Münk, my four-legged wonder and teacher of unconditional love.

Wendy Yao and Laura Owens make lemonade

A DINNER
Celebrating Lisa "Left Eye" Lopes'
MTV classic THE CUT
w/ cut recipes from this book

Family Style

Main Course
(3 Wines on table)

CHICKINNN

Chicken Chasseur Ballotine stuffed with wood-eared mushrooms & long cooked spigarello, smoked tomatoes mounted into chicken a tarragon heavy consume of clarified chicken jus

Pearl Morissette
Chardonnay
"Cuvee dix neuvieme, Niagara
2010

Cory Cartwright of Selection Massale
& Guilhaume Gerard

Squash SMOKED KABOCHA
w/ candied
by Guilhaume

On The Table

Ranch Waterfall
Crudite

Wine vinaigrette

H20—Saint—Geron

Domaine des marnes Blanches Savagnin "Cotes du Jura
2014

Dominique Belluard, perles du mont blanc, Haute Savoie

Crazy Sexy Gruel

Koda Farm Porridge with Jerk Beef Jerky, crispy onion, cardamom ghee

Jean Louis Dutraive Fleurie "Champagne" beaujolais
2014

Individually plated

Mung Bean Salad

Sprouted mung beans, roasted romanesco & brassicas, chocolate mint, cumin yogurt, pebre

Jochen Beurer, Kieselsandstein Riesling, Swabia
2012

DESSERT

INDIVIDUALLY PLATED

Almond Lemon Ricotta Cake Persian Mulberry Jam & Lemon Verbena Ice Cream

2014 Les Capriades "Piege a filles" Rose, Loire

DIN 4 LISA

To all the recipes that we lost you will 4ever b in our hearts